WINNING BASKETBALL

SECOND EDITION

TECHNIQUES AND DRILLS

FOR PLAYING BETTER

OFFENSIVE BASKETBALL

RALPH L. PIM, Ed.D.

McGraw·Hill

New York   Chicago   San Francisco   Lisbon   London   Madrid   Mexico City
Milan   New Delhi   San Juan   Seoul   Singapore   Sydney   Toronto

The McGraw·Hill Companies

Library of Congress Cataloging-in-Publication Data

Pim, Ralph L.
    Winning basketball : techniques and drills for playing better offensive basketball /
by Ralph Pim.—2nd ed.
       p.   cm.
    Includes index.
    ISBN 0-07-143000-8
    1. Basketball—Offense.   2. Basketball—Training.   I. Title.

GV889.P49   2005
796.323'2—dc22
                                        2004008001

2 3 4 5 6 7 8 9 0 FGR/FGR 3 2 1 0 9 8 7 6 5

ISBN 0-07-143000-8

Interior design by Think Design Group

Page 15: Figure from *Inner Strength: The Mental Dynamics of Athletic Performance* by Ralph A. Vernacchia, Pan Alto, California: Warde Publishers, Inc., 2003, p. 10. Used by permission from Warde Publishers, Inc.
Pages xvii and 1: Photos by Barry Gossage, NBA Photos. Used by permission from Basketball Communications, Phoenix Suns.
Pages 131, 135, 136, and 154–158: Photos by Dr. Lynn Fielitz, United States Military Academy. Used by permission.
All other interior photos by Gary Dineen. Courtesy of Marquette University.

McGraw-Hill books are available at special quantity discounts to use as premiums and sales promotions, or for use in corporate training programs. For more information, please write to the Director of Special Sales, Professional Publishing, McGraw-Hill, Two Penn Plaza, New York, NY 10121-2298. Or contact your local bookstore.

This book is printed on acid-free paper.

Dedicated to Coach Jack Greynolds

Coach Jack Greynolds was years ahead of his time. His pressure defense and up-tempo offense produced a style of play that devastated opposing teams and kept fans on the edge of their seats the entire game. One of his teams averaged almost 100 points a game for the entire season, and this was before the three-point shot. Basketball at Barberton (OH) High School was truly played with flair.

But Jack was more than an innovator and tactician. He was a leader that pushed his players to give their best at all times. He instilled a sense of pride in his players that still exists today. The skills he taught us on the court—teamwork, discipline, dedication, and perseverance—are the same tools that have helped all of us throughout our lives.

Coach Greynolds, thank you. You have given us memories and lessons that we will carry forever.

Contents

Foreword

Tom Crean, Head Coach, Marquette University

I consider it an honor and a privilege to write the foreword for *Winning Basketball*. I first met Coach Pim when I was a teenager growing up in Mt. Pleasant, Michigan, and he was coaching at Central Michigan University. He treated me with the same respect that he showed adults and spent hours answering my questions about coaching strategy, motivating athletes, and recruiting. Coach Pim has always been an important mentor to me.

I will always remember the day that Coach Pim gave me the opportunity to join his staff at Alma College. I was only 20 years old at the time, and I couldn't believe that he was asking me to coach on the collegiate level. Coach Pim's attention to detail and his ability to get the most out of his players led Alma College to its best overall record in 47 years. I treasure the memories of the three years we worked together, and I can never repay him for the opportunities he provided.

I learned from Coach Pim that the greatest thing a coach can do is to prepare his or her players for life after their playing days are over. Coach Pim built his teams on trust and respect. He demanded that his players work together and give their maximum effort. His respect and loyalty toward his players were unparalleled. Coach Pim wanted players to learn more from the game than just basketball skills. It is amazing to see the relationships that he still has with the players he coached. It speaks volumes not only about the type of coach that he was but, more important, about the kind of person Coach Pim is.

For the players reading this book, always remember the game of basketball is one of the greatest teachers in life there is. It teaches you first and foremost how to believe in yourself. You must develop physical and mental toughness in order to succeed because there are going to be many disappointments and setbacks along the way. You learn quickly that basketball is a team game. You must be unselfish and accept the role that helps your team the most. Basketball teaches you the importance of setting high standards and never accepting anything other than your best effort. Championship players have a blue-collar work ethic and strive to be better at the conclusion of every practice session. You also learn that having a positive attitude is essential to success. A great attitude led by an outstanding work ethic results in a commitment to excellence. I am a firm believer that you can't have people in your program who just want to win; you must have people who are committed to winning. Players that learn the value of hard work, commitment, teamwork, and sacrifice are the ones that make their teams great.

The foundation of your basketball game is your ability to execute the fundamentals in game situations. *Winning Basketball* can help you develop and improve your fundamentals because Coach Pim has done an outstanding job of presenting the key teaching points. The book provides drills and "Tips for Success" that will help elevate your game. Never underestimate the importance of fundamentals. Through hard work and repetition, your skills will improve.

For the coaches reading *Winning Basketball*, my advice is to demonstrate your love for the game every day and work to become a master at the art of teaching and coaching. Learn everything that you can and then apply it to your program. Read books, watch tapes, and talk and share information with other coaches. No coach ever stops learning. That's what makes the great coaches great. They strive to learn more every day and they never stop asking questions. Always remember the most rewarding aspect of the game is the impact that you can make in a person's life. If your players trust and believe in you, and they also know that you believe in them, they will move mountains for you.

The game of basketball is the epitome of what it means to grow and mature. Treat the game the right way and give it the respect that it deserves. Set high goals, work hard, and maintain a positive attitude and you will benefit in every area of your life.

In 2003, Tom Crean led Marquette University to their first Final Four in 25 years.

Acknowledgments

Every person who has ever touched my life both on and off the court has contributed to this book. A few deserve special mention:

My wife, Linda, for your loving support, patience, and understanding during many long days of writing. Thank you for all the happiness you have brought into my life. Life is beautiful with you.

Alissa and Stephanie. May your lives always be filled with love and peace. Live each day to its fullest and never forget the beauty of your dreams. I love you both dearly.

Kelly, Jason, and Sarah. Your optimism and enthusiasm for life brings great joy. Thanks for your love.

My sister, Mary Margulies and her husband David, for your love, support, and encouragement through the years. You have given so much, and I thank you with all my heart.

My parents, Alice and Lorin Pim, whose positive influence and daily examples instilled a sense of responsibility and shaped my optimism for life. You are missed dearly.

My assistant coaches, for your loyalty, work ethic, and commitment. I cherish the memories of our working together in pursuit of our dreams.

My players and students. There is nothing more satisfying than watching your successes.

I would like to thank the following people whose help was invaluable in the production of this book:

Mark Weinstein, editor at McGraw-Hill Trade

Katherine Hinkebein, project editor at McGraw-Hill Trade

Tom Crean, head basketball coach at Marquette University

Dan Majerle, former NBA player

John Farina, sports information director at Marquette University

Michael Broeker, assistant athletic director for media relations at Marquette University

Robin Jonathan Deutsch, director of New Media & Library Services at the Naismith Memorial Basketball Hall of Fame

Denny Kuiper, sports communication consultant and close friend

Barb Kellaher, coordinator of Men's Basketball Operations at Marquette University

Dwyane Wade, Robert Jackson, Scott Merritt, and Terry Sanders, former Marquette players

A special thanks to Dr. Lynn Fielitz, assistant professor at the United States Military Academy, for his expert editing and photography

Lyndi and Rachel Fielitz for demonstrating their ballhandling skills and allowing me to use their pictures

Dr. Ralph Vernacchia, sport psychologist at Western Washington University

Dr. Jerry Krause, director of Basketball Organizations at Gonzaga University

Julie Fie, vice president of Basketball Communications for the Phoenix Suns

D. C. Headley, manager of Basketball Communications for the Phoenix Suns

Introduction

Dan Majerle

If I were asked to describe my life in only three words, I would say that it has been "living a dream." I have experienced things in my life that at one time I could only dream about. The game of basketball provided an opportunity to play 14 years in the NBA. I played with great players and learned from some of the all-time best coaches. It also gave me the chance to represent our country in the Olympic Games and be a member of Dream Team II.

Most important, the game of basketball provided me with an opportunity to grow as a person. Never underestimate the importance of getting an education. Be a lifelong learner and use the game of basketball as a vehicle to make yourself the best person possible.

There are so many lessons that can be learned through your participation in basketball. Too often, athletes focus on winning championships, securing scholarships, or playing on television. These are all exciting accomplishments, but they are not the most important things in the long run. I believe the game of basketball provides an opportunity to learn lessons that can be carried over to everyday life. I can think of no better place to learn the value of hard work, persistence, teamwork, fair play, and sportsmanship.

My love for the game of basketball began many years ago. My father taught the fundamentals of the game to my brothers and me when we were youngsters growing up in Traverse City, Michigan. We spent the majority of our free time practicing basketball, and I'm sure our neighbors got used to hearing the sound of a bouncing ball coming from our backyard basketball court. It was a way of life at the Majerle house.

My parents encouraged us to participate in all sports. Their lives revolved around our practice sessions and games. Sports were the main topics of conversation at our dinner table, and my father always offered suggestions on how we could improve. My father was a good player in his day, and I can remember watching him play in independent leagues when I was a youngster. He wore No. 9, and that is the reason that I selected that number when I joined the NBA. In high school and college, I wore No. 44, but that number was worn by Paul Westphal and had been retired by the Phoenix Suns, so I selected my father's old number.

At Traverse City High School, I earned All-State honors in basketball and baseball and also was the quarterback on the football team. At Central Michigan University, I played both basketball and baseball. My younger brother, Jeff, who was a teammate of mine there, later played professional basketball in the Continental Basketball Association and in New Zealand. Steve, my older brother, was a standout on several nationally ranked teams at Hope College and is an outstanding high school basketball coach. In 2003, Steve led his team to the Michigan Class A state championship. His squad was only the second team in Michigan basketball history to win a Class A title undefeated.

I learned from my parents that it takes hard work to be successful. Everyone wants to be good, but very few people are willing to make the necessary sacrifices. Any success that I have attained has been the result of my desire and determination. I realized I had limitations, but I made a commitment to become the best player possible. To accomplish this I knew I had to work hard every day. I spent hours and hours developing my shot. Many times I had to shovel the snow off the court before I could practice. I skipped rope and did toe-raises to improve my quickness and jumping ability. I did push-ups in front of the TV to increase my upper body strength. I did ballhandling drills in the house to improve my dribbling skills. I was constantly searching for ways to improve.

It meant a lot to me in 2003 when the Phoenix Suns' CEO Jerry Colangelo described me as "a player who always gave the maximum effort" and established the annual Dan Majerle Hustle Award. It is awarded to the Phoenix Sun player who most typifies my game in terms of effort.

As a young player, I always tried to play against better competition. Fortunately, one of my high school coaches, Tom Kozelko, was an outstanding player at the University of Toledo and also played three seasons in the NBA. He taught me a lot about the game, and we would always play one-on-one after practice. That was a real learning experience— my skills developed much faster because of Tom.

In the NBA, playing against Michael Jordan was one of my greatest experiences because he was the best player in the league and the best player of all time. It was always a challenge. You knew that you had to raise your game to the highest level or Jordan would embarrass you. It was a fun challenge to have. Players should always look to play against the best players possible. It can be embarrassing at times, but it will help you improve your game.

My basketball idol growing up was Hall of Fame player Larry Bird. I enjoyed watching Bird because he did everything on the court to make his teammates better. He was an excellent passer, shooter, and defender. Bird loved the game of basketball and played hard every night. I pride myself in giving the maximum effort in everything I do. I was not the type of player who could go out on the court and coast. I never allowed someone to outwork me. When I was at Central Michigan, we were required to do a mile run prior to the start of the season. I won the race every year because I trained hard and refused to settle for anything less than first place. My pride would not allow me to lose.

At the 1988 Olympic trials, very few people knew that much about me. In fact no one knew how to pronounce my last name. I knew my intensity and aggressiveness were the key factors in making the team. I worked hard every second I was on the court. I never allowed the coaches to see me resting. I wanted to earn their respect and show them that I would do whatever was necessary to be successful. I made the squad and led the team in scoring and minutes played. It was a great experience playing for Coach John Thompson. It was also an honor representing the United States on Dream Team II and winning a gold medal.

In the game of basketball you are always faced with new challenges. Being selected the 14th pick of the NBA draft was an honor, but I knew that I had to raise the level of my game. On draft day many Phoenix fans booed when my name was announced as their team's first-round choice. I was sitting in my living room watching the draft with my family, and you could hear on the television that they were booing. Then Phoenix Suns announcer Al McCoy called and interviewed me on the radio and I could hear everybody in the background still booing. It didn't upset me because I knew they didn't have any idea who I was because I had come out of a smaller college. But I was determined to show them that the Suns had not made a mistake.

Cotton Fitzsimmons, head coach of the Suns, stood up and told the Phoenix fans that they would regret ever booing me. He watched me win the MVP at the Portsmouth Tournament after my senior year at Central Michigan and said that with my "heart and desire, there was no way that I would fail in the NBA." His belief in my abilities helped fuel my success during my rookie season in 1989. That particular team was the start of the Suns' rise to power. It was a great mix of veterans and young players.

I spent the first seven years of my NBA career with the Suns. We reached the Western Conference Finals three times and played the Chicago Bulls in the NBA Finals in 1993. The 1993 season was the most memorable in my career because we had the best record in the league and went all the way to the Finals.

I was disappointed when I was traded from Phoenix. It was no secret that I never wanted to leave. I loved Phoenix, and it's the place that I have made home.

The trade did provide opportunities for me, and one of those was the chance to play for Miami and Coach Pat Riley. I really enjoyed playing for Coach Riley because he demanded that all his players and coaches give 100 percent all the time. He did everything first class and took care of us. All he asked was for us to go out and play hard, be loyal, and do what he asked. My intensity and work ethic was a perfect match.

I feel fortunate that I had the opportunity to finish my career back in Phoenix. The Suns organization is like a family and they take care of people who played for them. It was an honor to be inducted into the Phoenix Suns' Ring of Honor. I joined playing legends Connie Hawkins, Dick Van Arsdale, Walter Davis, Tom Chambers, Kevin Johnson, Paul Westphal, Alex Adams, and former trainer Joe Proski. It is an honor that I will proudly carry with me my entire life.

Through the years, many rewards have come to me because of basketball. I have worked very hard and made many sacrifices, but I also have been very fortunate. I was able to make a living doing something that I truly love. I consider myself very lucky, and I hope I can put back into the game a small portion of what it has given me.

As you begin your basketball journey, my advice to you is quite simple.

Dan Majerle played 14 years in the NBA and participated in three NBA All-Star Games.

1. Enjoy every minute that you are playing the game. Basketball is the greatest game in the world. It provides an opportunity to learn lessons that will help you throughout your entire life.

2. Listen to your coaches. Your success depends on your ability to execute the fundamentals and work together with your teammates. Your coaches' feedback will help you improve and grow as a player.

3. Work hard. It takes hours of practice to develop your basketball skills. Don't become discouraged when things don't seem to work out. Your persistence is key to your success.

4. Respect the game and the people in the game. There have been thousands of coaches and players that have paved the road for your success. Learn from them.

My friendship with Coach Pim began when I was a junior in high school, and he recruited me to Central

Michigan University. He truly cares about the total development of his players, and I still have some of the letters that he sent to me when I was in high school. Coach Pim is an outstanding teacher and coach. He understands the game and has the ability to break down the fundamentals for easy comprehension and fast learning. This book is perfect for players who want to improve their game. I hope you enjoy *Winning Basketball*—I know it will help you on your quest for basketball success.

Key to Diagrams

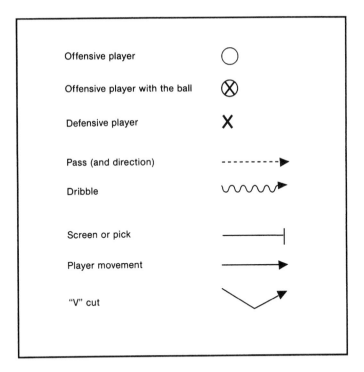

Offensive player	◯
Offensive player with the ball	⊗
Defensive player	X
Pass (and direction)	- - - - ▶
Dribble	∿∿▶
Screen or pick	———⊣
Player movement	——▶
"V" cut	⌄▶

Dreams Do Come True

"The future belongs to those who believe in the beauty of their dreams."

—Eleanor Roosevelt

The First Step

"Take the first step in faith. You
don't have to see the whole staircase, just take the first step."

—Martin Luther King Jr.

Congratulations! You have made an excellent choice in selecting this book, and you are ready to start your ascent toward becoming a successful basketball player. The journey will be challenging and rewarding. Step-by-step, you will increase your level of confidence and develop your basketball skills.

Definition of Success

Our first step is to examine the definition of success. Many people do not truly understand the meaning of success. They believe basketball success means playing professional basketball, obtaining financial security, or making an all-star team. Nothing could be further from the truth. Success is not measured by national recognition or financial rewards.

True success begins with focusing all of your resources on becoming the best player possible. It comes from knowing that you have given your best effort. Successful players strive to realize their potential.

In *Practical Modern Basketball*, Coach John Wooden defined success best when he said, "Success is peace of mind, which is a direct result of self-satisfaction in knowing you did your best to become the best that you are capable of becoming." The Wooden-coached UCLA teams reached unprecedented heights that will be difficult for any team to match. The Bruins set all-time records with four perfect 30–0 seasons, 88 consecutive victories, and 10 NCAA national championships, including 7 in a row.

Success Starts with a Dream

Becoming a successful athlete does not happen by accident. It takes planning, hard work, and continual assessment of your progress. The

Success starts with a dream.

first step in your journey is to visualize what you would like to accomplish. Pat Williams, senior vice president of the Orlando Magic, called this blue-sky thinking. He believed when people freed their imaginations, they would begin to see limitless horizons. Albert Einstein, the Nobel Prize winner, also understood the importance of imagination in his life and believed that imagination was more important than knowledge.

ACTIVITY 1.1: Identify Your Dream

1. Write down your dream.

2. List all the reasons why you want to achieve your dream.

Assess Your Basketball Skills, Attitude, and Work Ethic

To assist in your development as a basketball player, answer the questions in Activity 1.2 as objectively as possible. After recording your responses, ask your coach to answer the first three questions. Compare the results and identify your strengths and improvement areas.

ACTIVITY 1.2: Self-Assessment

1. List your two greatest strengths as a basketball player.

2. List your two weakest fundamentals as a basketball player.

3. What is your greatest asset as a team member?

4. How many hours per week do you spend practicing your basketball skills?

5. What percentage of your free throw attempts do you make?

For Questions 6–10, select the number, using the key below, that best reflects your opinion. Give specific examples to support your opinion.

5—Almost always
4—Most of the time
3—Sometimes
2—Seldom
1—Almost never

6. Are you confident about your future basketball performances?

　　　5　　　4　　　3　　　2　　　1

7. Do you take constructive criticism as an opportunity to learn, and do you learn from it?

　　　5　　　4　　　3　　　2　　　1

Continued

ACTIVITY 1.2: Self-Assessment, *continued*

8. Do you quickly regain your concentration after an error or a series of mistakes?

     5   4   3   2   1

9. Do you compliment and encourage teammates?

     5   4   3   2   1

10. Do you come to practice early (or stay after) and work on your weaknesses?

     5   4   3   2   1

The Power of Self-Image

The mental picture you have of yourself is called your self-image. A landmark discovery during the 20th century was the discovery of the self-image as a predictor of human behavior. Your self-image sets boundaries for your accomplishments by defining what you can and can't do. If you think you're not a good basketball player, you won't be. Winners see themselves as successful long before success actually happens because they have a positive self-image. You cannot consistently perform in a manner that contradicts the way that you see yourself. Your self-image will either lead you to the top or keep you from fulfilling your dream. There is no factor more important in life than the way you think about yourself.

Cultivate a Positive Self-Image

Positive thinking and goal setting will not work for you until you accept yourself and believe that you deserve success and happiness. Unfortunately, people with poor self-images always think success is for others, but not for them.

Now is the time to take control of your self-image. In *Wooden: A Lifetime of Observations and Reflections On and Off the Court,* Coach Wooden said, "Do not permit what you cannot do to interfere with what you can do." Focus on your strengths and do not let your limitations keep you from your dream.

Be prepared to overcome negativity and critics that diminish your talents. Remind yourself that you control your self-image and that no one can make you feel inferior without your permission.

Mental Training: Visualize Your Success

An important component in sports is a technique called mental training, or visualization. It is a strategy that involves using all the senses (sight, hearing, smell, touch, and taste) to create in your mind successful performance outcomes.

In *How to Be Like Mike* by Pat Williams, Michael Jordan explained how he used visualization to help him reach his dreams. "The successes I had didn't surprise me because I'd already experienced them in my mind," said Jordan.

To reach your dream, you must master the skills of the game of basketball. Visualization allows you to mentally practice skills correctly every time. Activity 1.3 provides an example of visualization using the free throw.

An excellent resource for mastering the techniques of visualization is *Inner Strength: The Mental Dynamics of Athletic Performance* by Dr. Ralph Vernacchia, sport psychologist from Western Washington University.

According to Vernacchia, "Seeing is believing and believing is the first step to achieving. A picture is worth 1,000 words. If we can see it, we can achieve it!"

ACTIVITY 1.3: Visualization

This exercise consists of 30 mental repetitions of your free throw. Perform 10 mental repetitions at game speed. Then perform 10 slow-motion repetitions. Finish with 10 mental repetitions at game speed.

1. Close your eyes and imagine you are at the free throw line preparing to shoot.

Continued

ACTIVITY 1.3: Visualization, *continued*

2. See the free throw line as you position your feet.

3. Hear the sound of the ball as it bounces off the court.

4. Feel the ball as you place your hands in the correct shooting position.

5. See the basket as you focus on your target.

6. Feel the movement of your arms and shoulders on the forward and upward thrust of the ball.

7. Feel the ball leave your fingers as you begin your follow-through.

8. Hold the follow-through, see the ball go into the basket, and hear the sound of the net.

9. Say "yes" at the completion of the made shot.

Set Specific and Measurable Performance Goals

Successful athletes have a clear understanding of what they want to accomplish. They establish short-range and long-range goals to help attain the desired end result. Goals serve as the road map to your dreams. Setting goals not only improves performance but also increases self-confidence and motivation.

Goal-Setting Guidelines

1. Set goals that are high enough to present a challenge but that still are within reach.
2. Focus on performance goals rather than outcome goals. Instead of setting a goal such as becoming a starter, focus on mastering specific components of skills that will lead to your outcome goal.
3. Set specific and measurable goals.
4. Write down your goals and place them in a visible place.
5. Continually evaluate your progress.
6. Stay flexible and adjust your goals when necessary.

ACTIVITY 1.4: Performance Goals

Based on the results of Question 2 in Activity 1.2, write two specific perfor-mance goals. Identify components of specific skills that will assist in your improvement. For example, if your free throw shooting is inconsistent because the placement of your shooting hand is not in the center of the ball, a specific performance goal would be: I will place the index finger of my shooting hand on the inflation hole during the preparatory phase of the free throw 8 times out of 10, or better.

Take Action

Your dreams will never become a reality unless you convert them into an action plan. Successful athletes design specific plans to reach their goals. Take time to chart your course. Identify practice times and spe-cific objectives for each practice.

Jordan reinforced the importance of adherence when in his book *I Can't Accept Not Trying*, he said, "You have to stick to your plan. A lot of people try to pull you down to their level because they can't achieve certain things. But very few people get anywhere by taking shortcuts. Very few people win the lottery to gain their wealth. It happens, but the odds certainly aren't with them. More people get it the honest way, by setting their goals and committing themselves to achieving those goals. That's the only way I'd want it anyway."

Most players have great intentions, but many do not adhere to their plan for one reason or another. Here are some suggestions that may help you adhere to your plan.

1. Surround yourself with people who want you to be successful. These individuals will support and encourage you during both the good and the bad times.
2. Find others who will work toward a common goal with you. Peer support is a strong incentive.
3. Use positive self-talk.
4. Monitor your progress by keeping a daily or weekly log.

5. Read your goals every day and visualize your success.
6. Place notes in your room or in your books to remind you of your goals for the day.
7. Rewards are a powerful tool. Reinforce your hard work and effort by giving yourself a reward.

Be Enthusiastic, Have Fun, and Learn How to Play

Basketball is a great game and should be enjoyed. Do not put such high expectations on yourself that you lose sight of the beauty of the sport.

The purpose of youth basketball leagues should be to help beginning players establish a strong basketball foundation. This foundation should consist of basic fundamentals, team play, sportsmanship, and an understanding of the rules.

Baseball legend Cal Ripken Jr. oversees Babe Ruth League's 5- to 12-year-old division and is concerned with the current state of youth sports. Ripken believes that youth baseball has overemphasized the importance of winning and failed to teach the right lessons.

Your practice time should be considered "special time" and an opportunity for you to grow both as a player and a person. Jordan's advice to young players is to enjoy playing and develop a love for the game.

As you practice, strive to improve your understanding of the skills that are necessary to become an effective player. Much of the enjoyment you derive from the game comes from your ability to experience success as you play.

Enthusiasm is paramount to success. Your love for the game should result in enthusiasm every time you take the floor. Enthusiasm is contagious. It is amazing how much energy and inspiration you can give to teammates when they see your passion for everything you do on the court.

TIPS FOR SUCCESS

1. Focus on becoming the best that you can be.
2. Start with a dream.
3. Continually assess your skills, attitude, and work ethic.
4. Remember your self-image is your blueprint for success.
5. Create goals that will serve as the road map to your dreams.
6. Set specific and measurable performance goals.
7. Enjoy playing the game of basketball.
8. Practice fair play and sportsmanship.
9. Be enthusiastic in everything that you do.

The Path to Excellence

"**Excellence is the gradual result of**

always striving to do better."

—Pat Riley, NBA champion coach

Many obstacles may stand between you and your dream. Every day you will make decisions that ultimately determine your success. This chapter will examine some of the qualities that are necessary to help you overcome these challenges.

Key Traits of Successful Performers

Why are certain athletes able to reach their goals while others do not? My experiences have shown that successful performers possess five key traits.

1. **Self-Respect.** Successful athletes value themselves as important and worthwhile. They hold themselves in high esteem, demonstrate respect for them-selves, and take pride in every-thing they do.

A postive self-image grows out of having strong character.

2. **Self-Responsibility.** Successful athletes take responsibility for their actions and their attitudes. They set goals and realize they must pay the price for success. They do not blame others for setbacks and are able to stay positive in difficult situations.

3. **Self-Confidence.** Successful athletes believe in themselves. They do not allow anything or anyone to diminish their self-worth. They look forward to competition because it is an opportunity for growth. They always give their best effort and trust in the results.

4. **Self-Improvement.** Successful athletes continually improve. They strive to master the skills necessary for success. They realize that basketball success is similar to climbing a never-ending staircase. There is always room for improvement and each new step presents new challenges.

5. **Self-Forgiveness.** Successful athletes are able to forgive themselves when they do not live up to their expectations. They understand they will experience setbacks and disappointments in their quest for success. They know how to get back up after they fall.

ACTIVITY 2.1: Work Ethic

What are your strongest traits or characteristics? If a person came into the gym and watched you play, how would he or she describe your attitude and work ethic? Identify one weak area. Establish a goal and develop a plan to improve in this area.

Top Factors Influencing Olympic Success

The United States Olympic Committee conducted a study of Olympians from 1984 to 1998 to identify the most important factors that contributed to their success.

According to the published results, the first factor recognized by Olympians was the importance of their inner drive, desire, persistence, and commitment to achieving their goals and to becoming the best that they could be. They possessed not only the dream but also the drive.

The second factor was the importance of family and friends. These individuals provided emotional and financial support, confidence, stability, and technical advice.

The third factor identified by Olympians was excellent coaches throughout their development. Coaches provided expertise, encouragement, and motivation.

Do everything to the best of your ability.

The Pyramid of Peak Performance

Dr. Ralph Vernacchia developed a peak performance pyramid to represent a systematic approach to achieve performance excellence (see Figure 2.1). He believed peak performers combined the personal attrib-

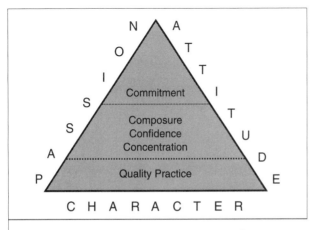

Figure 2.1 **The Pyramid of Peak Performance**

utes of attitude, passion, and character with the physical, mental, and emotional characteristics of commitment, confidence, concentration, and composure. Quality practice ties these elements together.

The Four Cs of Peak Performance

The four Cs of peak performance are commitment, confidence, concentration, and composure.

1. **Commitment.** Peak performers are relentless in their drive and determination to be the best that they can be. They hold themselves responsible for their actions and do not make excuses. They establish a reputation for giving 100 percent every time they go on the court.

2. **Confidence.** Peak performers are confident and approach competition with positive anticipation. They do not worry needlessly about their ability to perform. They have inner peace in knowing they have prepared themselves for competition and will always give their maximum effort.

3. **Concentration.** Peak performers are focused on the task at hand. They attend to the details of their performance and are able to quickly refocus when they get distracted.

4. **Composure.** Peak performers stay composed. They recognize potential threats to their overall performance and utilize strategies to refocus and perform at the highest level.

Stay completely focused on your primary purpose.

Taking Control

Successful performers focus on the things within their control. The two most important things that you control are your attitude and your work ethic.

Attitude

Your success depends on your attitude. Successful basketball players are optimistic and focus on the positive rather than dwelling on the negative. Find something positive in every situation and never allow problems to destroy your attitude. A positive attitude is the key to happiness in life.

Work Ethic

Never settle for anything less than your best effort. Many people do not reach their goals because they do not extend themselves. Successful performers exhibit a tremendous work ethic. They understand there are no shortcuts to success—it takes hours and hours of hard work.

Unselfishness

Basketball is a team game. Everyone must work together and get along in order to be successful. This does not mean that you have to be best friends with all of your teammates. But it does mean that you have to be willing to make sacrifices and fit within the structure of the team by playing a specific role. It is your responsibility to learn, accept, and play the role that will best help your team.

Arnold "Red" Auerbach led the Boston Celtics to eight straight NBA championships, a streak unmatched in professional basketball history. In *How to Be Like Mike*, Pat Williams quotes Auerbach: "Talent alone is not enough. They used to tell me you have to use your five best players, but I've found that you win with the five who fit together best."

It is amazing what a team can accomplish if no one cares who gets the credit. Selfishness will destroy a team.

Teamwork is the fuel that allows common people to attain uncommon results.

Perseverance

Basketball success does not happen overnight. Every player encounters setbacks throughout the course of a season or a career. Successful athletes have the ability to rebound quickly from mistakes and disappointments. They do not worry about things they cannot control. Once the play or game is over, they move on to the next challenge. They have the ability to stay positive and maintain their motivation during difficult times. Your true test will be how you handle adversity. Winners are survivors—they find a way to achieve success.

TIPS FOR SUCCESS

1. Demonstrate respect for yourself.
2. Take pride in everything that you do.
3. Take responsibility for your actions.
4. Improve every day.
5. Look for the positive in every situation.
6. View setbacks as opportunities.
7. Get back up after you fall.

Quality Practice

Practice Makes Permanent

"Practice is a privilege. If you're not

here to work, don't come."

—Dean Smith, Naismith Basketball
Hall of Fame coach

Improving your basketball skills requires hours of practice. Many times the difference between becoming a good player and a great player is *how* you practice. Do you practice just for the sake of practicing, or do you use practice time as a preliminary for peak performance on game night?

Every practice session provides an opportunity for self-improvement. It is your responsibility to make the most of this opportunity.

Basketball skills need to be practiced year-round—there is no off-season for a basketball player. The summer months are the best time for you to work on your individual skills.

Principles of Practice

To accelerate your growth as a player, adhere to the following principles of practice:

1. **Practice with a purpose.** Plan your practice time wisely. Decide in advance what to do, how to do it, and when to do it. Select drills and activities that will help you improve. Write down daily goals for practice sessions.
2. **Practice makes permanent.** Successful performers maximize their growth because they practice the fundamentals correctly. Pay attention to detail and master the fundamental skills of the game.
3. **Practice hard.** There is no substitute for hard work. Successful athletes are dedicated to becoming excellent players and push themselves to reach the next level.
4. **Practice smart.** Design your practice sessions so they are preparing you for competition. Going through drills at half speed does not prepare you for live game situations. You must practice as if it were a game. If no one is with you, pretend someone is guarding you. Use your imagination to create game conditions. Do not waste time practicing skills that you will never use in a game.

Practice sessions should be considered laboratories for learning. Players should come to practice with a "beginner's mind."

Masutatsu Oyama, the founder of the kyokushin-kai karate system, once said, "After 1,000 days of practice we are all beginners. After 10,000 days of practice we can only begin to understand the true meaning of our art." Master Oyama's statement can definitely be applied to the game of basketball. A player must understand that it takes years of practice before one can master the game.

Three Ps of Quality Practice

To aid in your development as a player, always adhere to the three Ps of quality practice.

1. **Be precise.** Successful athletes are precise in the execution of the fundamentals. They hold themselves accountable to the highest standard and do not take shortcuts.
2. **Be present.** Successful athletes stay in the present moment. They do not let past mistakes affect their game. They "see" the present and concern themselves with only those things they can control at that time.
3. **Be patient.** Successful athletes realize that patience is a virtue. Good things take time and there are many setbacks on the road to success. They believe that good things happen as a result of hard work.

Be precise in the execution of the fundamentals.

Repetition Is Essential

Your execution on game night depends primarily upon conditioned automatic reflex responses. You must practice a skill correctly again and again until it becomes automatic. Repetition is the best way to learn a skill so that it becomes a reaction at the instant you need it.

Incorporate Rest into Your Practice Schedule

Quality rest is essential for peak performance. Rest restores your energy and must be included in your practice schedule. Allow recovery time for your body after intense workouts.

Become a Student of the Game

If you really want to improve, study the game of basketball as you would study your favorite subject at school. The following techniques will help you understand the game and become a better player:

- Listen carefully to your coaches.
- Study the techniques of outstanding players.
- Watch videotapes of your play.
- Read instructional books.
- Mentally practice your basketball skills by using visualization.

In-Season Practice Guidelines

Good use of practice time during the season is essential for team success. Set daily goals and mentally prepare yourself before each practice. The following are practice guidelines that will help you become a better player:

1. **Be on time**. Be dressed, on the floor, and ready for practice on time.
2. **Stay focused.** Give your coaches your undivided attention. Listen carefully to instructions. Make eye contact with the person who is talking.
3. **Be positive.** Compliment teammates and be enthusiastic. There is no place on the court for complaining or criticism.
4. **Work hard.** Success comes from hard work. Give your best effort both physically and mentally.
5. **Hustle at all times.** There are no shortcuts. Practice at game speed and move quickly from

Listen carefully to your coaches and learn how to accept constructive criticism without looking for an excuse.

one drill to the next. Maintain your intensity and do not stop until you hear a whistle. Finish all plays.

6. **Believe in yourself.** You cannot become a great player without believing in yourself.

7. **Believe in your teammates.** Championship teams have players that believe and trust in each other.

8. **Overcome adversity.** You will be tested. Stay positive during challenging times and do not lose your self-confidence. A true test of champions is how they handle adversity.

Recognize your teammates for their accomplishments.

TIPS FOR SUCCESS

1. Practice with a purpose.
2. Practice hard and practice smart.
3. Set daily goals for your practice sessions.
4. Be precise—practice a skill correctly again and again.
5. Be present—practice in the present moment.
6. Be patient—remember success takes time and effort.
7. Incorporate rest into your practice schedule.
8. Mentally practice your basketball skills.
9. Remember: practice makes permanent.

Offensive Fundamentals

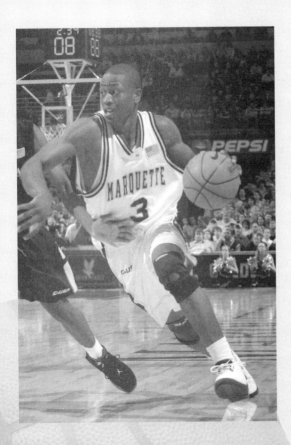

"I've never been much for Xs and Os and all kinds of fancy diagrams. Throughout my whole career I believed proper execution of the fundamentals separated the great teams from the also-rans."

—Arnold "Red" Auerbach,
Naismith Basketball
Hall of Fame coach

Balance, Quickness, and Offensive Footwork

> "The area of basketball that needs
>
> the most attention is offensive
>
> footwork and balance."
>
> —Pete Newell, Naismith Basketball
> Hall of Fame coach

Basketball is a game of balance and quickness. Before you can dribble, pass, or shoot effectively, you must move quickly and efficiently. You must be able to accelerate, change directions, and stop abruptly while maintaining your balance. Your ability to move while keeping your body under control will determine your basketball success.

Coach John Wooden considered two of the most important attributes of a player were quickness under control and team attitude. "Be quick—

Basketball is a game of balance and quickness.

but don't hurry" was one of Wooden's favorite expressions because he believed basketball must be played fast but never out of control.

It is also important to remember that your mental and emotional balance controls your physical balance. Do not lose sight of the importance of a balanced lifestyle. To maximize your basketball potential, set goals outside of your sport and do not neglect your family, academics, or friends.

Triple-Threat Position

The triple-threat position is the cornerstone of all offensive basketball fundamentals. It allows you to quickly shoot, pass, or dribble the ball.

After receiving a pass, first look at your basket. This allows you to see the floor and look for teammates that may be in a position to score. Quickly put the ball in the "shooting pocket," which is an area in front of your chest near your dominant shoulder. At the same time, square your body to the basket so that you are facing the rim and ready to make a quick offensive play. Many coaches call this action "catch and face."

The classic triple-threat position is as follows:

- Head is up and centered over the body.
- Eyes are looking at the basket and seeing the floor.
- Body weight is evenly distributed with the feet shoulder-width apart.
- Knees are bent.
- Shoulders are facing the basket.
- The ball is positioned near the dominant shoulder.
- Hands are placed on the ball in the shooting position. If you are within your shooting range, you must be an immediate threat to score.

The triple-threat position is the cornerstone for all offensive basketball fundamentals.

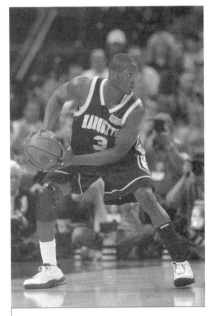

See the floor and look for scoring opportunities.

From the triple-threat position, you should look to do one of the following:

- Shoot.
- Pass inside.
- Pass on the perimeter to continue the offense.
- Dribble to create an open shot or pass.

To become an effective player, you must quickly get the ball into the triple-threat position after you receive it. A key teaching cue is "be ball quick."

Ready Position

When you do not have the ball, you should be ready to move quickly to receive a pass or help a teammate get open. The following points are helpful when playing without the ball:

- Keep hands above your waist and close to the body.
- Position your head directly above the rest of your body.
- Bend your knees.
- Keep your feet in contact with the floor as much as possible so that you are able to push off the balls of your feet and move quickly in any direction.
- Keep your eyes on the ball handler and your defender.
- Look for opportunities to help a teammate get open.
- Be ready to use a teammate's screen.

Starting

During the course of a game, players are continually accelerating from a stationary position. Quick starts can be improved by practicing the correct techniques:

- Lower your shoulder and lean your head in the direction you wish to go.
- Make the first step with the foot nearest the direction that you want to go.
- Push hard off the floor. The heel must come in contact with the floor on the push-off.
- Use your arms to accelerate by using a quick, pumping action.

Stopping

You must be able to stop abruptly in a balanced position. The two recommended ways to stop are the jump stop and the one-two stop.

Jump Stop

In the jump stop, both feet land simultaneously. The advantage of this type of stop is that you can then use either foot as your pivot foot. The jump stop is also called the *quick stop*. Some coaches prefer this term because it reinforces the teaching point that the feet stay close to the floor rather than jumping up into the air.

- Hop from one foot and stay close to the floor.
- Have both feet hit simultaneously.
- Land with the knees bent.
- Place feet shoulder-width apart.
- Keep the head up and centered over the body.
- Keep the back fairly straight.

One-Two Stop

In the one-two stop, the back foot lands first followed by the lead foot. The one-two stop can be used to change direction when running forward.

- Land the back foot first.
- Land the lead foot second.
- Stay low and keep your weight over the back foot.
- Keep the head up and centered over the body.
- Keep the back fairly straight.

Changing Directions

Offensive players must continually change direction in order to get free from their defenders. It is important to cut quickly, move in straight lines, and never cross your feet. The following are key teaching points when changing directions:

- Maintain a low center of gravity and keep your head centered over your body.
- Take a three-quarter step, plant your foot firmly, turn on the ball of the foot, and push off that foot in the direction that you want to go.
- Take a long step with the other foot. Your toes should point in the direction that you want to go.
- Lower your shoulder. Be low and explode.
- Have your hands up, ready to receive a pass.

Pivoting

Pivoting is the rotation of the body around one foot kept in a stationary position. You must become proficient pivoting with and without the ball. When you have possession of the ball and a pivot foot has been established, it cannot be lifted before the ball leaves your hand on a dribble. When shooting or passing, the rules allow you to lift the pivot foot as long as you release the ball before the pivot foot touches the floor again.

Pivot by turning on the ball of your pivot foot. Keep the ball close to your body as you pivot.

Pivoting is an essential skill because it allows you to move into an advantageous floor position. The two basic pivots are the front pivot and the rear pivot.

1. **Front Pivot.** The front pivot is executed by stepping forward while turning on the pivot foot. It can be used when your defender does not closely guard you.
2. **Rear Pivot.** The rear pivot is executed by stepping backward while turning on the pivot foot. It can be used when you are closely defended. The rear pivot is also called a *reverse pivot*.

The following are important points when executing either a front or a rear pivot:

- Maintain balance by keeping your feet shoulder-width apart and your knees bent.
- Keep your head up and centered over your body.
- Pivot by lifting up the heel and turning on the ball of your pivot foot.
- Protect the ball by keeping it close to your body with your elbows out.

Jumping

Jumping is an important skill in the game of basketball. Your ability to jump can be improved by increasing the strength of your leg muscles and by using the correct techniques for jumping.

Your ability to jump quickly is more important than the height of your jump. Hall of Fame coach Fred Taylor from Ohio State believed that the best players had the ability to make successive jumps because they landed with balance and were able to go back up in the air quickly.

The following are key teaching points for jumping:

- Anticipate the jump.
- Start in a balanced position with the knees bent.
- Take a short step prior to the takeoff.
- Push quickly and forcefully off the floor.
- Swing the arms upward.
- Land on the balls of your feet with your knees flexed.
- Be prepared to make second, third, and fourth efforts.

How high you can jump is not nearly as important as your positioning and timing.

TIPS FOR SUCCESS

1. Remember basketball is a game of balance and quickness.
2. Anticipate and be in a ready position.
3. Be quick without hurrying.
4. Keep your knees bent.
5. Be aware that the position of your head controls your balance.
6. Keep your hands above the waist.
7. Catch and face.
8. Be ball quick.
9. Be a triple-threat every time you catch the ball.

Perimeter Shooting

"If you can't put the ball through the

hoop, you are not going to win

many ball games against the teams

that can."

—John Wooden, Naismith Basketball
Hall of Fame coach

Shooting is the most important fundamental in the game of basketball. Regardless of how well a team does everything else, if it cannot score points it will not be successful. The offensive fundamentals of passing, dribbling, and rebounding may enable a team to get shooting opportunities, but then players must be able to make the shot.

Shooting also is the most enjoyable and most practiced fundamental in the game of basketball. Everyone wants to become a better shooter. It is exciting to score points. All players dream of making the game-winning basket or being the leading scorer on their team, but it takes hours and hours of practicing the correct shooting fundamentals to develop the ability to score under pressure. Great shooters vary somewhat in their styles, but their shooting techniques are fundamentally sound. Understanding and implementing the correct shooting techniques is essential for success in this game.

Be Eager to Learn

The first step to becoming a great shooter is an eagerness to learn. A player must be willing to listen and take constructive recommendations from coaches who are experts in the area of shooting. It takes tremendous desire and dedication to become an outstanding shooter.

Perfect Practice Makes Perfect

The old saying "practice makes perfect" can be improved by the addition of a single word: "*perfect* practice makes perfect." This definitely is the case in shooting. Players must practice the correct fundamentals in order to become outstanding shooters.

A player who has a smooth, free-flowing shot is often called a pure shooter. This soft shooting touch is not a natural gift. Outstanding shooters are made, not born. Players must always remember that shooting is a skill that is developed through practicing the correct fundamentals.

The Formula for Shooting Success

Great shooters perform the skill without conscious thought. It is an automatic response that develops through dedicated practice.

Dick Parfitt, former coach at Central Michigan University, believed the formula for shooting success was C + C = B.

$$\text{Concentration} + \text{Confidence} = \text{Basket}$$

Concentration

- **See it.** Focus on the target with every shot attempt and see the ball going into the basket.
- **Feel it.** Pay attention to the details of correct shooting and feel the body movements necessary to produce a successful shot.
- **Trust it.** Perform in the present and let go of any missed shots in the past.

Confidence

- Believe in yourself as a shooter.
- Remember the shots you made—not the ones you missed. Analyze your misses and then forget about them.
- Picture yourself as a successful shooter.
- Develop confidence with hours and hours of perfect practice.

Basic Mechanics of Perimeter Shooting

There are many important fundamentals involved in shooting a basketball. Following are the key points to becoming an outstanding shooter.

Balance

- The shot starts on the floor. The feet must be ready and the body is flexed at the knees and the waist. The knees are flexed in order to give power to the shot.
- Feet are shoulder-width apart with the weight evenly divided. The foot on the same side of your body as your shooting hand is slightly in front.

Good shooters exhibit concentration and confidence.

- Head is kept over your feet. There is no lateral or backward movement of the head. The position of your head affects the center of gravity and controls your balance. The head must be kept level and straight.
- Ball is held in the shooting pocket (triple-threat position). Always bring the ball into the shooting pocket after receiving a pass or picking up the dribble. This places the fingers in an upward position.

Sight

- Eyes are focused on the target before, during, and after the shot attempt. Maintain a narrow focus either on the imaginary center of the rim, on back of the rim, or on the upper corner of the backboard rectangle.
- Do not lift the head up to watch the flight of the ball.

Grip for the Shooting Hand

- The index finger of the shooting hand is centered and placed directly behind the ball. A point of reference is that the shooting index finger should point at the inflation hole.
- The fingers of the shooting hand are spread comfortably, with the ball touching the whole hand except for the palm.
- The forefinger and the thumb of the shooting hand form the shape of the letter "V." The thumb is kept relaxed to avoid tension in your hand and forearm.

All shots must be balanced.

Grip for the Nonshooting Hand

- The proper position of the nonshooting hand, called the balance hand, has been one of the most neglected areas in shooting. In order to have a smooth release, both hands must work together.
- The balance hand is kept either on the side or slightly under the ball. The weight of the ball balances on the fingers, primarily on the ring finger and little finger to avoid the common mistake of the thumb push.
- The nonshooting hand serves only to balance the ball, not to shoot it. It is moved slightly out of the way as the shot is released.

Square to the Basket

- Squaring the body to the basket is essential to shooting success.
- Toes are pointed at the basket. The big toe of the shooting foot should be pointed directly toward the center of the rim.
- The head is in line with the center of the target.

The shooting hand is centered on the ball and the fingers are spread comfortably.

Using the balance hand properly is very important, because the ball must slide smoothly up through the fingers during release of the shot.

Shooting Alignment

- The alignment of the hand, wrist, elbow, shoulder, and feet in relation to the basket determines the line of flight of the ball.
- To shoot the ball in a straight line, the shooting foot, shoulder, elbow, wrist, and hand must be on the same line with the basket throughout the entire shot.
- The shooting alignment should never vary from one shot to the next. The main emphasis in shooting practice is to develop a grooved shot where the shooting arm stays in the correct line on every shot.

Elbow Alignment

- Proper alignment of the elbow is a must for high-percentage shooting.
- The shooting elbow is kept up and in so that the ball is aligned to the basket. There is a slight diagonal slant from the elbow to the hand with the emphasis on keeping the elbow in.

- The elbow is closer to the target than the wrist—this will ensure that the ball is cocked properly and avoids "pushing" the ball to the basket.

Shooting Rhythm

- Excellent shooters have a smooth and fluid motion that begins with the feet and extends through the fingertips on the follow-through.
- The legs initiate the shot, and the toes are used as springboards. The energy in your legs establishes your shooting rhythm. A quick, strong upward push off the floor is

Keep your shooting elbow in and properly aligned with your hand and wrist.

essential for quickness and range in perimeter shooting. This quick push is more important than the depth of the knee bend.

- Get the ball into the proper shooting alignment as quickly as possible.
- Lock the wrist and cock it back. The back of the hand is approximately parallel with the floor. You should see wrinkles on the back of your wrist when the ball is cocked properly. Cocking the ball in the shooting pocket is called "loading the gun."
- The ball is brought straight up past the face. The shooting elbow is lined up with the shooting foot. The ball must be taken straight up. A common mistake made by many shooters is throwing the hips forward and the shoulders back.
- Thrust the ball up and forward with the fingers. The elbow is used like a hinge.

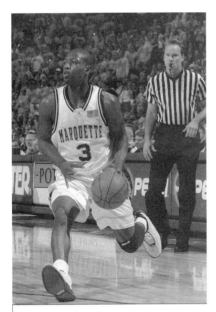

Square your body to the target and push forcefully straight up off the floor.

After bringing the ball up into the shooting pocket, take it straight up past your face and cock your wrist.

The ball is lifted, as the fingers are thrust up and forward through the ball.

Direct your arm, wrist, and fingers straight toward the basket and release the ball at a 60-degree angle.

- The ball is released near the top of the jump. As the wrist snaps, the ball is released off the thumb, index, and middle fingers.
- Release the ball high. The best angle of release for shooting is 60 degrees above horizontal.

Follow-Through

- The follow-through is necessary to ensure proper arc and ball rotation. The ball should be released so that it has a slight backspin. This assures that the ball will travel

The ball rolls off the fingers as the wrist snaps.

in a straight line. It also deadens the rebound effect if the shot is missed.

- There is complete elbow extension and wrist flexion during the follow-through. After releasing the ball, the palm of your shooting hand should face down.
- Hold your arm in the follow-through position until the ball reaches the basket. This is a critical fundamental because it will keep you from pulling your arm back too quickly. Think of it as "posing for the cameras" for at least one second after the ball is released.
- To get the correct follow-through, visualize reaching into a cookie jar that is positioned on a high shelf or putting your hand into the basket at the completion of your shot attempt.
- Land balanced and ready to move.

The BEEF Principle

The fundamentals of shooting can be remembered using the acronym BEEF.

There is complete elbow extension and wrist flexion during the follow-through. Hold the follow-through and stay balanced as you return to the floor.

- **Balance.** Begin and end every shot on balance. The majority of shots are missed because of poor balance. Point your feet at the basket, shoulder-width apart with your shooting foot slightly ahead. Take the ball to your shooting pocket with the fingers pointed upward. Keep your head centered over your body and go straight up on your jump shot.

- **Eyes.** Concentration is one of the keys to successful shooting. Keep the same sighting point on all shots. Either focus on the imaginary center of the rim, back of the rim, or the upper corner of the backboard rectangle. Maintain your vision on the target before, during, and after the shot attempt.

- **Elbow.** The position of your elbow is key to developing the correct shooting alignment. The shooting elbow should be up, in, and under the ball. Legendary coach Clair Bee used the phrase "elbow squeeze" to emphasize the correct position of the elbow. Bee told his players to always squeeze the elbows in when you are getting ready to shoot.

- **Follow-Through.** The shooting arm is extended at the elbow and flexed at the wrist. Hold the follow-through position until the ball reaches the basket.

All-American Dwyane Wade Demonstrates Shooting Excellence

First Team All-American Dwyane Wade recorded Marquette's first triple double since 1994 with 29 points, 11 rebounds, and 11 assists as he led the Golden Eagles to an 83–69 victory over the number one–ranked Kentucky Wildcats in the 2003 NCAA Regional Finals. It sent Marquette to its first Final Four since 1977.

In Photos 5.1 through 5.8, Wade demonstrates a series of well-executed offensive fundamentals that produced two of his team-high 19 points against Kansas in the national semifinals.

The Miami Heat selected Wade as the fifth overall pick in the 2003 NBA draft. During his rookie season, Wade was named the NBA's Eastern Conference Player of the Week and played in the Rookie Game during the NBA All-Star weekend.

Photo 5.1 **Shot Fake—Dwyane Wade uses a shot fake to get his defender off the floor. Notice how Wade's knees remain bent as the ball is brought up.**

Photo 5.2 **Ball Quickness—As the defender goes for the fake, Wade brings the ball down quickly in preparation for his dribble penetration.**

Photo 5.3 **Long First Step—Wade creates space from his defender by taking a long first step on his dribble drive. Notice how Wade keeps his eyes focused on the basket.**

Photo 5.4 **Legs Initiate Shot—Wade brings the ball to his shooting hand, squares his body to the basket, and prepares for a powerful push off the floor to initiate the shot.**

Photo 5.5 **Load the Gun—Wade brings the ball straight up past his face and cocks his wrist in preparation for the shot.**

Photo 5.6 **Balance and Concentration—Wade begins the forward thrust of his shot while maintaining perfect balance.**

Photo 5.7 **Forward Thrust—Wade's fingers are thrust up and forward through the ball. The ball rolls off the fingers near the top of his jump.**

Photo 5.8 **The Follow-Through—There is complete elbow extension and wrist flexion during Wade's follow-through. Notice how Wade maintains his vision on the target.**

Perimeter Shooting Self-Assessment

Shooting practice provides an opportunity for you to assess your shooting mechanics. Every shot provides instant feedback. An understanding of the correct shooting fundamentals and your body's ability to "feel" these movements is crucial to shooting success.

One of the best ways to identify your shooting strengths and weaknesses is to videotape your shooting form. Shoot 100 shots from a spot on the floor that is within your shooting range. Videotape 25 shots from each of the following angles: (1) back view; (2) side view on the shooting hand side; (3) side view on the balance hand side; and (4) front view.

What to Look for When You Videotape Your Shot

Back View

- Feet are shoulder-width apart with the weight evenly divided.
- The head is straight and not leaning to one side or the other.
- The index finger of the shooting hand is positioned in the center of the ball.
- The fingers of the shooting hand are spread evenly.
- The index finger and thumb of the shooting hand form the letter "V." One of the worst mistakes is spreading the thumb and the index finger too far apart. This will tighten the muscles on the back of the hand, creating an uneven force on the shot.
- The balance hand is positioned on the side of the ball with the fingers evenly spread.
- The shoulders are square to the basket.
- The shooting elbow is up, in, and under the ball.
- The elbow, wrist, and hand are aligned throughout the shot.
- The ball has backspin on its path to the basket.
- The shooting hand and wrist stay on a straight line to the basket during the follow-through. Check the position of the shooting arm on the follow-through to make sure it is not going either to the right or left.

Side View (Shooting Hand Side)

- The shooting foot is slightly ahead of the balance foot.
- Knees are flexed slightly.
- The head is straight, level, and directly over the rest of your body.
- The fingers of the shooting hand are pointed upward when the ball is in the shooting pocket.
- The shooting arm can be in the low, medium, or high elbow lift position.
- The ball is taken straight up from the shooting pocket to the cocked position.
- The head is straight. Watch carefully to make sure the head is not moving backward as the shooter brings the ball up.
- When the ball is in the cocked position, the back of the shooting hand is approximately parallel to the floor and the elbow is ahead of the ball.
- The shoulders, hips, and feet are aligned over the top of the other.

- The ball is thrust forward with the fingers. Make sure the shooting elbow is not overextended and locked.
- The ball is released just before or at the top of the jump. The best angle of release for shooting is approximately 60 degrees above horizontal.
- Eyes stay on the target and do not follow the flight of the ball.
- During the follow-through, the shooting arm is extended at the elbow and flexed at the wrist. The fingers of the shooting hand are pointed downward. Hold the follow-through position until the ball reaches the basket.

Side View (Balance Hand Side)

- The balance hand grips the ball on the side or slightly under the ball.
- The ball slides up through the fingers of the balance hand during the forward thrust.
- The ball is released near the top of the jump.
- The fingers of the balance hand point upward on the release.

Front View

- The feet are shoulder-width apart, with toes facing the basket.
- The ball is brought straight up.
- The body is square to the basket.
- The shooting elbow is kept up and in during the shot.
- The balance elbow is held out rather than under the ball to improve the shooter's vision.
- The target is seen with both eyes. Make sure the ball does not block the shooter's vision.
- On the follow-through, the fingers of the balance hand point upward and the fingers of the shooting hand point downward.
- The follow-through is held for at least one second.

Chart Your Misses

An excellent method to evaluate your shooting technique is to chart your misses. Shoot 100 shots, and for all your misses, have your partner record the location on the rim where the ball initially hit. By analyzing the location of your missed shots, you can detect and correct your shooting errors.

Correcting Perimeter Shooting Errors

The most common perimeter shooting errors are listed below along with possible reasons.

Common Mistakes When Shooting the Ball Right or Left

- The shooting elbow, wrist, and hand are incorrectly aligned.
- The body is not square to the basket.
- The feet are not pointing toward the basket.
- The shooting hand is not centered on the ball.
- The balance thumb is propelling the ball on the shot.
- The index finger and thumb of the shooting hand are too far apart or too close together.
- The index finger and thumb of the balance hand are too far apart.

Common Mistakes When Shooting the Ball Short

- The ball is released on the way down rather than near the top of the shooter's jump.
- There is too little push off the floor during the initiation of the shot.
- The feet are spread too far apart, diminishing the power generated from the push off the floor.
- The arms are overextended back over the head before the forward thrust.
- The ball is not being thrust forward on the shot so the wrist cannot supply power to the shot.
- The shooter does not follow through with the shot.

Common Mistakes When Shooting the Ball Long

- The shooting arm releases the ball on too flat a trajectory. The best angle of release for shooting is 60 degrees.
- The arms are overextended in front of the body prior to thrusting the ball forward. The ball should be held in the shooting pocket and brought straight up.
- The shooting hand and the balance hand are too far apart.
- The shooting arm is not completely extended on the shot.
- The shooter pushes forward when jumping off the floor instead of straight up.

Common Mistakes for Inconsistent Shooting

- The shooting elbow, wrist, and hand are incorrectly aligned.
- The ball is cocked over the shoulder rather than in the shooting pocket.
- The ball is cocked too far back over the head.
- The head moves backward during the forward thrust of the shot.
- The elbow is positioned out from the body.
- The shooter does not follow through with the shot.
- The ball is cocked a second time before the release. Once the ball is cocked, the shooter should not cock it again.
- The ball is released off the ring finger instead of the index or middle finger. This gives the ball sidespin rather than backspin.

Footwork Prior to Shooting

Many coaches and players underestimate the importance of footwork prior to shooting. Footwork is the key to getting the shot off quickly and maintaining balance. A quick, forceful push off the floor provides power to the shot. The result is a faster, smoother shooting rhythm and a quicker release on the shot. With proper footwork, it is much easier to get into the correct shooting alignment. Two types of footwork that can be used from a pass or a dribble are the one-two stop and the one-count stop.

Footwork Facts

- The speed of your shot is determined by fast footwork. Do not have lazy feet!
- The rhythm initiated by the footwork should be carried through the entire shot. Do not try to speed up or slow down the upward thrust and release of the ball because the shot will lose its flow.
- The height of the jump is not as important as how fast you initiate the shot with your feet and how quickly you get yourself into the correct shooting alignment.
- Practice the proper footwork as fast as possible without losing balance or rhythm.

One-Two Stop

- The one-two stop is executed by placing your inside foot down first. The key is to put the heel and the inner side of the foot down first. This allows you to come up off the floor easily on the ball of your foot.
- The toes of the inside foot are aimed at the basket.
- It is normally best to take a smaller step going into the one-two stop because it provides greater balance.
- Bring your outside foot forward and square your body to the basket. The outside foot should be placed so that your feet are approximately shoulder-width apart. The shooting foot is positioned slightly ahead of your balance foot.
- Push off the floor with both feet as you initiate the shot.
- When shooting off the dribble, coordinate the last dribble with the one-two step. Lower the inside shoulder as the body is turned into the shooting position.

One-Count Stop

- The one-count stop is executed by landing on both feet at the same time. The one-count stop is recommended because it is quicker than the one-two stop.
- Jump slightly from your inside foot and land with your feet approximately shoulder-width apart, pointed at the basket. Your shooting foot is slightly ahead of your balance foot.
- Use a quick, forceful hoplike motion.
- When shooting off the dribble, coordinate the last dribble with the last step on your inside foot. This should be a hard dribble in order to quickly place the ball in the "shooting pocket"—in front of your chest near your dominant shoulder.

Shooting off the Dribble

Players must learn how to shoot accurately off the dribble. To accomplish this you must maintain body balance as you combine dribbling skills with proper shooting fundamentals. You must also pick up the ball off the dribble using the same grip whether you are dribbling to your strong-hand side or your weak-hand side. Correct hand position helps ensure proper release on the shot. There are several key fundamentals when shooting off the dribble.

- While dribbling, have the knees bent and legs ready to push off the floor quickly.
- Push the ball down hard on your last dribble.
- Pick the ball up facing the basket. Your shoulders must be square to the basket.
- When dribbling to the strong-hand side, pick the ball up in front of your shooting knee with your shooting hand. Bring the balance hand over to the ball. No grip adjustment should be needed as you bring the ball up to the shooting pocket.
- When dribbling to the weak-hand side, execute a quick crossover dribble to your shooting hand. Pick up the ball in front of your shooting knee and bring the balance hand over to the ball. No grip adjustment should be needed as you bring the ball up to the shooting pocket.

Shot Selection

Successful teams generally shoot a higher field goal percentage than their opponents. For this to happen, each player must understand proper shot selection. Knowing when not to shoot is just as important as knowing when to shoot. One of the more difficult tasks of a coach is teaching shot discipline. Coaches can assist players in learning their shooting range by keeping accurate statistics and charting shooting drills. Follow these guidelines for shot selection.

Be Within Your Shooting Range

- For two-point field goal attempts, your shooting range is that area in which you can make at least 50 percent of your shots.
- For three-point field goal attempts, your shooting range is that area in which you can make at least 33 percent of your shots.

Have a Good Look at the Basket

- Shooters must be well balanced and have a good look at the basket.
- Avoid shooting when closely defended. A hand in your face significantly lowers your shooting percentage.

No Teammate Has a Better Shot

- You must see the floor and look for open teammates.
- If a teammate has a better shooting opportunity, pass the ball to him or her.

The Rebounding Areas Are Covered

- Avoid perimeter shots when your teammates are not close to the basket.
- It is important that you have teammates in the proper rebound position in case the shot is missed.

The Score and Time Indicate a Need for This Shot

- What may be a good shot at one point in the game may be a bad shot at another point.
- Shot selection is always decided by the score and the amount of time left to play.

Three-Point Shooting

During the past 20 years nothing has changed basketball as much as three-point shooting. A three-pointer is psychologically the most powerful play in the game—it demoralizes the defense and is the quickest way to build your own team's momentum. Overall, the three-point shot has brought tremendous excitement to basketball.

Today, players are shooting three-pointers more than ever before. Over 32 percent of the shots attempted in college basketball are from three-point range, and three-point baskets account for approximately 27 percent of the scoring at this level. As a result, three-point shooting has become a key component in the offensive and defensive strategies of all coaches.

The three-point shot has placed an even higher premium on shooting. Every team has a place for the player that can hit the three-point shot. Becoming a successful three-point shooter takes time and practice. Follow these guidelines for three-point shooting.

Know Where the Three-Point Line Is at All Times

- Never take a shot when stepping on the line.
- Spot up in the three-point area in your early offense.
- Relocate to a three-point shooting area after feeding the post.

Be Ready to Shoot the Three-Point Shot

- Get your hands up and be ready to receive the pass.
- Bend your knees and get your legs ready to initiate the shot.

Always Be Moving Toward the Basket on the Shot

- Never take a shot falling away from the basket.
- Step into your shot and use your legs to increase your shooting range.
- Shoot the ball on the way up rather than at the top of your jump.

Be Balanced and Under Control

- Maintain the proper alignment and use the correct shooting mechanics. Your hand and arm motions are the same on all perimeter shots.
- Develop a shooting rhythm utilizing your legs, back, and shoulders.

Hold the Follow-Through

- Maintain vision on the basket before, during, and after the shot.
- Hold the follow-through position until the ball reaches the basket.

TIPS FOR SUCCESS

1. Be on balance when you shoot.
2. Be square to the basket.
3. Initiate the shot with your legs.
4. Place your shooting hand in the center of the ball.
5. Load the gun.
6. Keep your shooting elbow up and in.
7. Develop a smooth shooting rhythm.
8. Keep your head still.
9. Hold the follow-through.
10. Follow the "BEEF" principle.
11. Practice game shots at game speed.

6

Layup Shooting

"You should make 100 percent of
your layups. The only reason not to
make a layup should be that you
were so severely fouled that your
shooting motion was interrupted."

—Oscar Robertson, Naismith Basketball
Hall of Fame player

The layup shot should be the highest percentage shot in the game of basketball. Unfortunately many layups are missed due to lack of concentration. Your primary focus must be on making the shot as quickly and as efficiently as possible. A soft shooting touch is a prerequisite for success. You must also become proficient at shooting with either hand so that the ball can always be kept away from the defender.

Fundamentals of the Layup Shot

Your first priority in shooting a layup is to put the ball in the basket. You must be aware of your driving angle to the basket, how closely you are guarded, your speed, and the defender's height and jumping ability. Adhering to the following fundamentals will help you become an outstanding layup shooter.

- Keep the head up and concentrate on the target.
- Dribble with the hand away from the defense.
- Bring the nondribbling hand to the ball so that the ball is kept away from the defender.
- Take the ball up with two hands for protection.
- Jump off the foot opposite the shooting hand, driving the other leg and knee up and toward the basket. You should "high-jump" toward the basket rather than "long-jump."
- Release the ball at the top of the jump.
- Use the backboard when driving to the basket from the wing.

Keep your head up with your eyes focused on the target.

Shoot the ball softly off the backboard.

- Shoot the ball softly off the board, hitting the top corner of the backboard square. You should shoot the ball "high and soft" off the backboard.
- When driving down the middle of the floor or from the corner, shoot the ball over the top of the rim using the underhand layup.

Types of Layups

The layup is the most basic shot in the game, and there are five basic types you can use depending on the shooting situation.

Overhand Layup

The overhand layup should be used in situations when you are closely defended or when you have beaten your defender and have time to lay the ball in the basket. The overhand layup is a difficult shot to block.

- The shooting hand is centered and positioned on the back of the ball.
- The nonshooting hand is placed on the side of the ball.
- Your shooting knee is lifted as you jump off the inside foot.
- The ball is brought up with both hands to a point between the ears and the shoulders.
- The palm of your shooting hand faces toward the backboard and the back of your shooting hand faces your body.
- You extend the elbow and flex the wrist and fingers forward.
- The ball is released by a slight flick of the wrist, fingers, and elbows.
- You see the ball go in the basket after taking your shot.

Underhand Layup

The underhand layup should be used in situations when you are approaching the basket at high speed or when you have driven past a defender on your way to the basket.

In the overhand layup, the palm of your shooting hand faces the backboard and the back of your hand faces your body.

- As you reach your high-est point on your jump, the ball is extended upward and away from the body.
- The shooting hand is in front and under the ball.
- The palm of your shooting hand faces toward your body and the back of your hand faces the basket.
- The fingers of your shooting hand point upward.
- The ball is released with a slight turning and flicking of the wrist and fingers.
- The ball appears to roll off the fingers.
- You see the ball go in the basket after taking your shot.

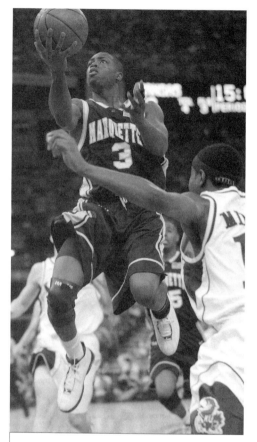

The shooting hand is in front of and under the ball in the underhand layup shot.

Power Layup

The power layup is used when you are closely defended inside the lane.

- Come to a jump stop with your shoulders parallel to the baseline.
- Point the toes toward the baseline.
- Grip the ball firmly with both hands.
- Take the ball up with two hands for protection.
- Jump off both feet and keep your body between the ball and the defender. Do not expose the ball to the defense.
- Shoot using the hand away from the defensive player.
- Use the backboard.

Reverse Layup

The reverse layup is used when you are forced under the basket and come out the other side for a shot. It is also used after securing a rebound or loose ball under the basket.

- This is a difficult shot to block because you use the rim for protection.
- Your back faces the basket at the time of the shot.
- The head is tilted backward and the eyes are focused on the basket.
- You jump off the foot opposite your shooting hand.
- The ball is taken upward with both hands.
- The palm of the shooting hand faces the basket, and the ball is shot in front of and above the head.
- A gentle flick of the wrist is used to flip the ball back and bank it off the backboard.
- You see the ball go in the basket after taking your shot.

One-Hand or Two-Hand Breakaway Dunk Shot

Players who can make the dunk shot can use either the one-hand or two-hand breakaway dunk shot. The most important thing is to finish the play and score two points.

- Be aggressive and attack the basket. The dunk shot is one of the most exciting plays in basketball. It can serve as a great momentum builder when executed successfully.
- Jump off the foot opposite of the dunking hand.
- Hold the ball with both hands from the time you pick up your dribble to the point when you begin the dunk.
- Hold the ball firmly. It is difficult to maintain control if the ball is held in your fingertips.
- Go up strong and maintain your focus on the rim.
- At the highest point of your jump, be sure your arm is extended.

Jump off both feet and keep the shoulders parallel to the baseline when taking the power layup shot.

The reverse layup is tough to block because the rim is used for protection.

- Throw the ball through the rim by snapping your wrist quickly.
- After scoring, think immediately of your defensive responsibility. This is not the time to celebrate or showboat.

When shooting a breakaway dunk, go up strong and maintain focus on the rim.

The dunk shot is one of the most exciting plays in basketball.

Practicing Layup Shots

Even though the layup shot is the most basic shot in basketball, most players do not practice it enough. Never take layups for granted. They must be practiced every day. Some players "hear footsteps" and lose their concentration when defenders are sprinting after them. For other players, the fear of getting hit by a defender disrupts their shooting rhythm on the layup shot.

Practice layups coming in from different angles. Become proficient shooting with either hand and always go at game speed.

Become proficient using either hand when shooting layup shots.

TIPS FOR SUCCESS

1. Keep your head up.
2. Concentrate on the target.
3. Dribble with the hand away from the defense.
4. Bring your nondribbling hand to the ball.
5. Take the ball up with two hands.
6. Jump off the foot opposite from your shooting hand.
7. High-jump rather than long-jump.
8. Shoot high and soft off the backboard.
9. Become proficient using either hand.

Free Throw Shooting

"I've never really understood why more players don't make the effort to become good free throw shooters. It just takes practice and hard work. And concentration."

—Larry Bird, Naismith Basketball
Hall of Fame player

Points scored from free throws make up a large percentage of the total point production. In college basketball, approximately 21 percent of a team's points are scored from the free throw line.

Practice, Practice, Practice

The free throw line is the perfect place to help your team because most close games are decided by free throw shooting. Surprisingly, however, many players do not spend enough time practicing their free throws.

Through hours of practicing the correct shooting fundamentals, you can improve your free throw percentage. NBA star Karl Malone wasn't a good free throw shooter when he entered the NBA—in fact, he made only 48 percent of his free throws during his rookie season. But as a result of hard work and dedication, Malone improved his free throw shooting percentage to 79 percent.

Hall of Fame player Earvin "Magic" Johnson made 79 percent of his free throws during his freshman year at Michigan State University. By his 10th season in the NBA, Johnson had improved his free throw shooting to more than 91 percent. When asked how he did it, Johnson simply replied that he practiced by shooting 150 free throws a day.

Establish a free throw routine based on sound shooting fundamentals.

Develop a Positive Shooting Attitude

You should be excited every time you get fouled because you know that you will score points for your team. You must go to the free throw line confident. The free throw is the only shot in basketball that remains the same on every attempt. Focus on your target, believe in yourself, and block out all distractions.

An excellent resource to help you reach your potential and become a better free throw shooter is *Beyond the Absolute Limit* by Stan Kellner.

Establish a Free Throw Routine

The best way to improve your free throw shooting is to establish a routine that you follow on every attempt regardless of the situation or score. Routines vary from player to player, but the end result is a consistent technique.

The first step is to establish a free throw routine that prepares you both mentally and physically for the shot. It gives you something to focus on rather than the pressure of the moment, and it allows you to "feel" the shot going into the basket even before you shoot the ball. Once you have established a free throw routine that works for you, believe and trust in your system. Do not alter or change your routine.

The following recommendations will help you develop a successful free throw shooting routine:

1. **Say an affirmation statement as you go to the free throw line.**
   - An affirmation statement motivates you for success and eliminates negative self-talk.
   - Silently repeat a positive phrase such as "Yes! My shot is great" or "Nothing but net."

2. **Place your feet in the correct shooting position.**
   - Feet are approximately shoulder-width apart.
   - Shooting foot is directly in line with the basket.
   - Balance foot is several inches behind the shooting foot.

3. **Visualize the ball going through the basket.**
   - "See" the ball going through the basket.
   - Say to yourself trigger words such as "yes" or "swish" as you visualize the ball going through the net.

4. **Bounce the ball a set number of times.**
   - Find the inflation hole on the ball.
   - Keep your eyes on the inflation hole as you bounce the ball.

5. **Establish the correct hand position on the ball.**
   - Use the inflation hole as a guide. Point the index finger of your shooting hand at the hole.
   - Always have your shooting hand in the correct position.

6. **Bring the elbow in.**
   - Feel your elbow move in and under the ball.
   - Use the correct elbow position to establish the proper alignment for the shot.

7. **Bend the knees.**
   - The shot begins with your legs.
   - Establish a consistent knee bend on all shots.

8. **Concentrate on the target.**
   - Focus on the basket.
   - See a "large" target. Remember, two balls can fit through the basket at one time.

9. **Extend the shooting arm in a smooth, fluid motion.**
   - Bring the ball straight up past your face.
   - Your elbow is used like a hinge as you thrust the ball up and forward with the fingers.

10. **Release the ball high.**
    - Release the ball when the arm, wrist, and fingers of the shooting hand are fully extended.
    - Feel the ball roll off your fingers. Snap your wrist slowly and smoothly.

11. **Hold the follow-through.**
    - After the ball is released, the palm of the shooting hand should face down.
    - Hold your arm and hand in the follow-through position until the ball reaches the basket.

Keep your elbow under the ball and extend your shooting arm in a smooth and fluid motion.

Be confident, maintain your focus, and use the correct fundamentals when shooting free throws.

The importance of concentrating on your target and holding your follow-through until the ball goes through the net cannot be overstated.

Hold your follow-through until the ball reaches the basket.

Practice Free Throws Under Game Situations

Always try to practice free throws under gamelike conditions. Shoot free throws after running sprints or when you are tired. Establish drills that simulate late-game situations and imagine that you are shooting game-winning free throws.

Desired Free Throw Shooting Percentage

The national average for free throw shooting in college is 69 percent. Goals for free throw shooting accuracy should be set according to age and ability level. The following free throw shooting percentages are general guidelines:

Desired Free Throw Shooting Percentage

LEVEL	PERCENTAGE
Elementary	50
Middle School	60
Senior High School	70
College	75

TIPS FOR SUCCESS

1. Practice free throw shooting every day.
2. Prepare yourself to shoot pressure free throws.
3. Establish a routine. Do the same thing on every shot.
4. Believe and trust your system.
5. Visualize the ball going in the basket.
6. Place your feet in the correct shooting position.
7. Place your shooting hand in the center of the ball, using the inflation hole as a reference point.
8. Keep your elbow in.
9. Initiate the shot with your legs.
10. Shoot the ball in a smooth, fluid motion.
11. Release the ball high.
12. Hold your follow-through.

Passing and Catching

"It doesn't matter who scores

the points. It's who gets the ball to

the scorer."

—Larry Bird, Naismith Basketball
Hall of Fame player

Passing is the foundation for teamwork and scoring. Next to shooting, it is the most important offensive fundamental. Defensive players have difficulty reacting to good passes. Consequently, good passing teams end up with high-percentage shots.

There was a time in basketball when passing was actually in danger of becoming a lost art—good passers were a rarity. But in the 1980s, future Hall of Fame players Earvin "Magic" Johnson and Larry Bird brought a new dimension to the game with their outstanding and creative passing.

Fundamentals of Good Passing

Passing is the quickest way to advance the ball. The first step to becoming a good passer is learning how to use peripheral vision to "see" the court. In their book *Basketball According to Knight and Newell*, legendary coaches Bob Knight and Pete Newell said, "When you face the basket with the ball, you have to 'see.' Anyone can 'look.' But it takes a player to 'see' what is going on. Seeing the game involves three things: recognition, anticipation, and execution."

It is the passer's responsibility to determine if the receiver is open. To pass successfully, you need to see your potential receivers and their defenders.

Passing is the second most important offensive fundamental.

Good passers "see the floor" and look for open teammates.

1. **See your receivers.** Recognize their floor position and readiness for a pass. Anticipate any cutting action or movement.
2. **See the defenders.** See the floor position of the defensive player guarding the potential receiver. Recognize the amount of pressure your defender is applying.

Create Open Passing Lanes

Good passers create open passing lanes. A passing lane is the area between two offensive players where a pass could be made. Your objective as a passer is to create a passing lane that is free of defenders.

Two ways to open passing lanes are by dribbling and faking.

Dribbling

When your defender plays loosely, one method of opening a passing lane is by dribbling. A sagging defensive player has too much time to react to the pass after it has been thrown. Dribbling toward the defender will freeze that player and allow a pass to be completed.

Good passers create open passing lanes.

Dribbling also may be necessary to create a passing lane when the defender plays the ball handler tightly. A quick dribble to either side will get the defender out of the passing lane and establish a better passing angle.

Faking

Faking is another technique used to open a passing lane. Read the defender's arm position and create an opening for a pass to a teammate. If the defender's arms are up, fake low and then pass high. If the defender's arms are down, fake high and then pass low.

Principles of Passing

Whereas excellent shooters make only 50 percent of their shots, good passers should be almost 100 percent effective. Here are the principles of passing and key teaching points:

1. **Be accurate.**
   - Pass the ball to a spot where your teammate can do something with it.
   - On perimeter passes, aim for the shooting pocket.
   - See both the defender and the hands of your potential receiver.
   - Always throw the ball to the side away from the defender.

Use fakes to throw the ball past your defender.

Throw crisp, quick passes by snapping your wrists on the follow-through.

2. **Throw crisp, quick passes.**

   - Always put "zip" into your passes by snapping your wrists on the follow-through.
   - Do not wind up when you pass the ball.
   - Take a quick step in the direction of the pass.
   - Keep two hands on the ball until you release the pass.
   - Pass the ball quickly, before the defender has time to react.
   - It is your responsibility to throw passes to teammates that you know they can catch.

3. **Deliver the ball on time.**

   - You must anticipate the speed of your receiver on any cut.
   - The pass must be delivered when the receiver is open.
   - A late pass is a poor pass.

4. **Use deception and fakes to open passing lanes.**

   - It is difficult to pass around a defender that is playing off the ball. Close the distance between you and your defender and then use fakes to get the defender's hands out of position.
   - Fake in one direction and pass in the opposite direction.
   - Don't "telegraph" your pass. See your target without looking directly at your receiver.

5. **Pass ahead to an open player.**

   - Always look to pass ahead to an open player.
   - Do not force a pass or throw the ball ahead to a teammate who is not in a better floor position than you are.

The ball should be passed ahead to an open teammate whenever possible.

Catching

Passing and catching go together—you cannot have a successful pass without a successful reception. Very often players and coaches do not spend time practicing the fundamentals of catching, and many turnovers are caused by a lack of concentration by the receiver. Here are key points to remember when catching a pass:

1. **Give the passer a target.**
   - Keep your hands up.
   - Show the passer where you want the ball thrown.

2. **Meet each pass.**
   - Move toward the ball until contact is made.
   - Cut toward the pass or take a step and reach for the ball.

3. **Watch the ball into your hands.**
   - Concentrate on the flight of the ball.
   - Do not take your eyes off the ball. A teaching cue to emphasize is "look the ball into your hands."
   - Do not begin your next move before actually catching the ball.

4. **Catch the ball with two hands.**
   - Do not attempt to catch the ball with one hand.
   - Relax your fingers and thumbs prior to catching the ball.
   - As you make contact with the ball, allow your hands and arms to give toward your body.
   - After catching the ball on the perimeter, always square up to the basket and put the ball in the triple-threat position, as explained in Chapter 4.

Types of Passes

From the two-hand chest pass to the baseball pass, there are a variety of passes good players use depending on the game situation.

○ **The receiver must concentrate on the flight of the ball and catch the ball with two hands.**

○ **For ball movement, the chest pass is effective and efficient.**

Two-Hand Chest Pass

The two-hand chest pass is the most effective and efficient pass for ball movement. It is used to get the ball to a teammate when there is no defender in the passing lane. Key teaching points when using the two-hand chest pass are:

- Position the ball in the center of your chest. Keep it close to your body.
- Hands are placed on both sides of the ball.
- Place thumbs behind the ball.
- Bend the body forward and step toward the receiver.
- Release the ball by extending the elbows as the thumbs turn down and the palms rotate outward.

- Push the thumbs through the ball to produce backspin.
- Snap your wrists on the follow-through.

Two-Hand Bounce Pass

The two-hand bounce pass is often used at the end of a fast break or when passing to a player in the post or to a player making a backdoor cut. A shot fake or high-pass fake usually precedes a bounce pass.

Remember—the bounce pass is the slowest of all passes. A cardinal rule in passing is never throw a crosscourt bounce pass from one guard position to the other because the pass is easily intercepted and often results in a layup shot for your opponent. The key teaching points for the two-hand bounce pass are:

- Use the same grip as for the two-hand chest pass.
- Bend the body forward and step toward the receiver.
- Release the ball by extending the elbows as the thumbs turn down and palms rotate outward.
- Push the thumbs through the ball to produce backspin.
- Snap your wrists on the follow-through.
- The ball should bounce at a point about two-thirds of the distance between the passer and the receiver.
- The receiver should catch the ball waist-high.

Overhead Pass

The overhead pass is used when you have to pass over your defender. It is very effective against a zone defense because it allows the ball handler to pass from one side of the court to the other. It can also be used as an outlet pass to initiate a fast break or to feed the post. Key teaching points for the overhead pass are:

- Hold the ball directly above your head. Do not bring the ball behind your head because it takes longer to throw the pass.
- Grip the ball with the fingers pointed upward and thumbs on the back of the ball pointing inward.
- Step forward with the pass.
- Thrust both arms forward. Keep your elbows slightly flexed during the throw.

- Release the ball with a quick snap of the wrist and fingers.
- At the completion of the pass, your fingers should face the target.
- The receiver should catch the ball at chin level.

One-Hand Push Pass

The one-hand push pass is used to pass through players or past a defender who is guarding closely. It can be a direct pass or a bounce pass and is often preceded with a vertical fake (example: fake high, pass low). Listed below are key teaching points when using the one-hand push pass:

- Start in the triple-threat position with one hand behind and the other hand on the side of the ball.
- Use a quick push and wrist snap to provide the force of the pass.
- Release the ball past the defender.

The overhead pass is released with a quick snap of the wrist and fingers.

Baseball Pass

The baseball pass is used as a long pass to a cutter breaking toward the basket. It is also used to inbound the ball quickly after a score. This is a difficult pass to control, and accuracy is very important.

- Keep your body parallel to the sidelines.
- Position the passing hand behind the ball while the other hand is in front and slightly under the ball.
- Plant the rear foot and step with the front foot toward the receiver.
- Keep two hands on the ball as long as possible.
- Throw the ball from behind the ear with the force provided by a quick wrist snap and arm thrust.
- Follow through with full pronation and extension of the arm.

Behind-the-Back Pass

A more advanced skill, the behind-the-back pass can be used in a fast-break situation when two offensive players are attacking one defender. It is a very effective pass as long as it is used in the right situation. It can be either a direct or a bounce pass.

- Turn your body toward your passing arm side.
- Keep both hands on the ball as you move it to a position behind your hip.
- Cup the ball in your throwing hand.
- Swing your throwing arm in a circular path around the body and behind the back.
- Provide the force of the pass by a whip of the arm and by finger flexion on the release.
- Point your fingers at the target on the follow-through.

TIPS FOR SUCCESS

Passing

1. See the floor.
2. Create open passing lanes.
3. Put "zip" on your passes.
4. Throw accurate and timely passes.
5. Pass ahead to open teammates.

Catching

1. Give a target.
2. Catch with both hands.
3. Look the ball into your hands.
4. Give with the pass. Have soft hands.
5. Catch, face the basket, and be a threat.

Dribbling

"Whatever position you play, whatever your size, you must be able to dribble if you want to be a complete basketball player."

—Oscar Robertson, Naismith Basketball Hall of Fame player

Dribbling is one of the basic fundamentals of the game and is an integral part of team play. Dribbling is one method of advancing the ball to create scoring opportunities.

For beginning players, dribbling is probably the most misused and overused fundamental. Former Central Michigan University coach and athletic director Ted Kjolhede compared dribbling to eating candy by saying, "A little bit is good, but too much will make you sick."

Beginning players often tend to over dribble and not gain any advantage over their defenders. Young player also make the mistake of dribbling the ball once immediately after catching a pass, thus wasting their dribble. Players must learn to always dribble with a purpose.

Dribble with a Purpose

Successful basketball players use dribbling to create scoring opportunities. Before beginning the dribble, assess the situation by looking at your basket, seeing both your teammates and their defenders. Use the dribble to move the ball into a better floor position. Never put the ball on the floor unless you have a reason to dribble. Use the dribble to:

- Advance the ball up the court.
- Drive toward the basket.
- Improve a passing angle.
- Get out of trouble.

Key Points When Dribbling

1. **Keep your head up.**
   - Dribble without watching the ball. Dribbling is a touch skill.
   - See the entire floor and look for open teammates.

Keep your head up and always dribble with a purpose.

Keep your nondribbling arm up for protection.

- Focus your attention on the basket. A teaching cue that emphasizes this point is "eyes under the net."

2. **Dribble skillfully with either hand.**
   - Become a proficient dribbler with either hand so that you can dribble in any direction and your defender cannot overplay you.

3. **Dribble with the hand farthest from the defender.**
   - Always protect the ball.
   - Keep your body between the ball and your defender.
   - Keep the nondribbling arm up for protection.

4. **Never pick up the dribble without a pass or a shot.**
   - Once you start your dribble, keep it alive until you pass or shoot. This is a cardinal rule for dribbling.
   - Picking up your dribble allows defenders to pressure you because they no longer have to worry about dribble penetration.

5. **Do not dribble into trouble.**
   - Use your dribble wisely.
   - Do not dribble between two defenders or into the corners of the court.
   - Be alert for traps.

How to Dribble

The placement of your hand on the ball and fingertip control are keys to controlling your dribble. The following are important teaching points in executing the dribble:

- The dribbling hand should be cupped and the fingers spread comfortably.
- The dribble is a push-pull motion of the arm, wrist, and fingers. Initiate the dribble by elbow extension and flexion of the fingers and wrist.

A cardinal rule of dribbling is once you begin your dribble, do not pick it up until you pass or shoot.

- Your wrist should be kept flexible. Beginning players often make the mistake of dribbling with their entire forearm and keeping their wrist stiff.
- The forearm serves as a rudder and helps steer the ball in the direction that you want to go.
- Your fingers should meet the bouncing ball, with your wrist absorbing the upward force.
- The fingers and the pads of the hand control the ball. The palm of your hand should not touch the ball. Remember, fingertip control is essential to become an effective dribbler.
- You should dribble the ball with a quick, firm bounce. Be careful not to have a "lazy" dribble.

Practice dribbling with your hand on each of the following areas of the ball: directly on top, in front, behind, on the right side, and on the left side. This develops excellent ball control and prepares you for a variety of dribble moves that you can use to outmaneuver defenders.

Types of Dribbles

You should become skilled using each of the following types of dribbles.

Control Dribble

Use the control dribble when you are closely guarded. Protect the ball by keeping your body between the ball and the defensive player.

- Dribble the ball at knee level or lower.
- Use a staggered stance with the ball-side foot back.
- Advance the ball with a step-and-slide movement.

The hand is cupped, the fingers are spread comfortably, and the fingers and the pads of the dribbling hand control the ball.

When using the control dribble, advance the ball with a step-and-slide movement and always keep your body between the ball and your defender.

When using the speed dribble, keep your body nearly erect, leaning slightly forward. Dribble the ball near waist level or higher to gain maximum speed.

- Keep the free arm up for protection.
- Keep the elbow of the dribbling arm close to the body.

Speed Dribble

Use the speed dribble in the open court to advance the ball quickly.

- Keep your body nearly erect, leaning slightly forward.
- Extend your dribbling arm fully, pushing the ball out in front of your body.
- Dribble the ball near waist level or higher to attain maximum speed.

Retreat Dribble (Pull-Back Dribble)

The retreat, or pull-back, dribble allows you to maintain your dribble against defensive pressure. It is used to create space from a defensive trap or a run-and-jump situation. The retreat dribble is often combined with a crossover dribble.

- Keep your head up so that you can see the floor.
- Control dribble at knee level and keep the nondribbling arm up for protection.
- Create space from a defensive trap by using short, quick retreat steps while dribbling backward.
- Maintain your balance and look to either pass to an open teammate or change direction with your dribble.

Change-of-Pace Dribble (Hesitation Dribble)

Use the change-of-pace dribble to penetrate past a defender. Its purpose is to make the defensive player believe that you are slowing down. When your defender relaxes, drive quickly toward the basket. Continue dribbling with the same hand and in the same direction as before the hesitation.

When using the change-of-pace dribble, straighten up slightly, throw your head up to relax the defensive player, and then accelerate quickly past the defender.

- When slowing down, plant your lead foot, straighten up slightly, and throw your head up to relax the defender.
- Accelerate quickly by pushing off the ball of your lead foot.
- Use a low dribble to go past the defender.

Crossover Dribble

Use the crossover dribble to make a sharp change in direction. It can be especially effective when you are being overplayed. The advantage of the crossover dribble is that you never lose visual contact with the basket and your teammates. The disadvantage is that you may expose the ball to your defender if you are being guarded too closely.

- When the foot on the dribbling side contacts the floor, push off hard toward the opposite foot.
- Slide the dribbling hand to the outside and top of the ball.
- Force the ball across your body on a low diagonal path with a flick of your wrist and fingers. Use a quick, hard bounce.
- Reach down with the receiving hand to get the ball on a short hop at the same time as you take a step with the foot on that side.
- Your receiving hand should be cupped and should give slightly when it receives the ball.
- Complete the move with a long crossover step by the foot on the original side of the dribble.

Spin Dribble (Reverse Dribble)

The spin dribble is also called the reverse dribble. Use the spin dribble to change direction when you are closely guarded and the crossover dribble is too dangerous to attempt. The advantage of the spin dribble is that your body is always between the ball and the defender. The disadvantage is that you momentarily lose visual contact with the basket and your teammates.

- When initiating the spin dribble with a right-hand dribble, stop with the left foot forward and pivot on the ball of the left foot.
- At the same time, "pull" the ball close to your body with the right hand until you complete the pivot and make the first step with your right foot.

When using the spin dribble, pivot on the ball of the foot, "pull" the ball close to your body, and switch the ball to the other hand after you have completed your rear turn.

- After completing the rear turn, switch the ball to the opposite hand.
- Turn your head quickly in order to see the floor.

Behind-the-Back Dribble

The behind-the-back dribble is another way to change direction. This technique is safer than the crossover dribble and quicker than the spin dribble. Another advantage of the behind-the-back dribble is that you always maintain visual contact with the basket.

- When you initiate the behind-the-back dribble with your right hand, have your weight on your right foot and dribble the ball close to your hip.
- Push the ball with a quick flick of the wrist and fingers and a whipping motion of the lower arm.
- As you move your left foot forward, bounce the ball behind your back and into your left hand, continuing the dribble.

Between-the-Legs Dribble

Use the between-the-legs dribble to force a defender off balance so you can penetrate toward the basket. It is an effective dribble when you are being overplayed.

- Keep the ball low and dribble from one hand to the other.
- Force the ball through your legs with a quick, hard flick of the wrist and fingers and a whipping motion of the lower arm.

Inside-Out Dribble

The inside-out dribble is a fake change-of-direction maneuver that is used to create a drive to the basket or a shot.

- As you dribble toward your defender, initiate the inside-out dribble by crossing the ball to the midsection of your body.
- At the same time, use a head fake to make your defender move backward or laterally.
- Quickly, rotate the position of your hand on the ball and bring the ball back to the side from which you started.
- Look to drive to the basket or pull up for a jump shot.

Dribble Penetration

Nothing hurts a defense as much as dribble penetration. Whenever the ball gets inside the defense, the result is normally a high-percentage shot for the offensive team.

In basketball today, the premier guards create scoring opportunities for themselves or their teammates through dribble penetration. Two keys in dribble penetration are getting past your defender and finishing the play.

Getting Past Your Defender

The first step is finding a way to get past your defender. Excellent ball handlers are able to create openings that enable them to drive to the basket. To accomplish this

When using the between-the-legs dribble, use a quick, hard flick of the wrist and fingers to dribble from one hand to the other.

Dribble penetration really hurts a defense. When the ball gets inside, the result is often a high-percentage scoring opportunity.

objective, a dribbler must get his or her defender out of the driving line (an imaginary straight line from the ball handler to the basket).

1. **Faking.** One way to open the driving line is by using fakes. When a dribbler is closely guarded, an effective fake will move the defender off the driving line. This creates an opening to drive. The faking technique could be a foot fake, such as a jab step, or it could take the form of a head fake or ball fake.

2. **Dribbling.** A second way to create an open driving line is by dribbling. Any of the dribbling moves—the crossover, spin, behind-the-back, between-the-legs, or the inside-out dribble—can be used to get past the defender. When the defender is in a sagging position, the dribbler should gain momentum by dribbling right at the defensive player before executing a dribble move. It is difficult for a stationary defender to contain a penetrating dribbler.

Outstanding penetrators see their teammates and create scoring opportunities.

Finishing the Play

Outstanding penetrators must keep their heads up, see their teammates as well as their defenders, and never dribble into trouble. NBA legend John Stockton was one of the best point guards at finishing plays after penetrating past his defender. After getting past your defender it is essential to read the situation correctly and finish the play.

1. **Penetrate and score.** When the driving line is free of defenders, penetrate to the basket and score.
2. **Penetrate and pitch.** When the defender of a teammate positioned on the perimeter picks you up, pass to the open player for a perimeter jump shot.
3. **Penetrate and dish.** When a post defender steps up to stop you, pass inside to your open teammate.

TIPS FOR SUCCESS

1. Dribble with a purpose.
2. Think pass first; dribble second.
3. See the floor. Dribble without looking at the ball.
4. Dribble skillfully with either hand.
5. Use fingertip control.
6. Keep your body between the ball and the defender when closely guarded.
7. Never pick up the dribble without a pass or a shot.
8. Be able to change speeds and directions when dribbling.

Perimeter Moves

"Too often a player decides what move he will make before he receives the ball. This is often a mistake. Reading and reacting to the defender must be stressed."

—Pete Newell, Naismith Basketball Hall of Fame coach

Individual moves are an important part of a team's offense if they are used in an unselfish manner. All players must learn to work together and use individual moves to create the best scoring opportunities for their team.

Perimeter Play Principles

Every time you catch the ball on the perimeter, remember to do the following:

- Look at your basket.
- Bring the ball into the triple-threat position.
- Square up to the basket.
- Read the defense to determine whether to shoot, pass, or dribble.

Reading the Defender

In order to make the best possible offensive move, you must quickly analyze your defender's floor position. The defender's most vulnerable side is the front foot because he or she must make a pivot before being able to recover and stop the dribbler. Rather than looking down at your defender's feet, observe which hand is up since in a normal defensive stance, the hand that is up will be on the same side as the lead foot.

- When the defender is in a staggered stance and has one hand up, attack the side with the hand up.
- When the defender leaves the floor or plays with straight legs, penetrate to the basket.
- When the defender backs up, take the perimeter jump shot.
- When the defender rushes at the ball, drive to the basket.
- When the defender reacts to a jab step by moving laterally, penetrate in the opposite direction from the fake.

Faking

Faking is a technique used to get a defensive player off balance or out of position. To be effective, a fake must look like the real thing. Fakes by a ball handler are designed to open passing lanes, create shots, or open driving lanes to the basket.

An offensive player can use ball fakes, shot fakes, foot fakes, head fakes, and eye fakes to deceive a defender. Many times you need to use a combination of fakes in order to gain an advantage. Generally, players fake in one direction and move in the opposite direction.

Remember the following points when using fakes:

- Ball quickness is essential when making pass fakes and shot fakes.
- Use your eyes to look in the same direction as the fake.
- When using foot fakes, always fake into the defensive player as much as possible.
- When using shot fakes, do not straighten your legs. When the ball goes up, stay down and keep your knees bent.

One-on-One Moves

Every player likes the challenge of playing one-on-one. There is tremendous satisfaction in driving past your opponent and creating a scoring opportunity either for yourself or a teammate. Perfecting the following moves will help you beat a defender in a one-on-one situation.

Direct Drive

The direct drive is used to penetrate past a defender. No fake is necessary with the direct drive because you have a driving lane to the basket. The first step is crucial. It must be a long, quick step with the foot opposite the pivot foot.

When using the direct drive, take a long, quick step with your nonpivot foot.

- Push off the pivot foot.
- Take a long, quick step with the nonpivot foot.
- Accelerate past your defender by pushing the ball ahead. Work on getting distance with your first dribble.
- Keep your head up and see the floor.

Jab Step and Jump Shot

A jab step is a short, quick step directly at your defender with the nonpivot foot. If the defensive player respects the jab step and moves backward with the hands down, quickly bring the jab-step foot back and shoot a jump shot.

- Jab step at your defender.
- When your defender moves backward and keeps both arms down, quickly bring the jab-step foot back into a balanced shooting position.
- Shoot the jump shot.

Hesitation Move (Jab Step, Long Step, and Drive)

If the defensive player does not move on your jab step, take a long step past the defender. This long step is called a power step. As a general rule, anytime you get your foot even with the defender's foot or your head and shoulders past your defender, drive past the player.

- Jab step at your defender.
- If the defender does not react to the jab step, immediately push off the pivot foot and take a long step past the defender.

Anytime you get your head and shoulders past your defender, drive past the player.

Crossover Step and Drive

The crossover step is used when you are overplayed. It consists of a short jab step followed by a crossover step with the same foot. The ball is brought quickly across your chest as you step past your defender's lead foot.

- Make a short jab step at your defender's front foot.
- When the defender reacts to your jab step and moves laterally to block your path, quickly execute a crossover step with the same foot.
- Cross over with a long step past your defender's foot.
- At the same time, swing the ball quickly across, keeping it close to the body.
- Keep your inside shoulder between the defender and the ball.
- Keep the pivot foot stationary while you make the jab step and the crossover step.
- Push the ball ahead on the floor and drive.

Rocker Step and Drive

The rocker step can set up either a drive or a shot from the perimeter. It is used when the defender reacts to a foot fake by moving either forward or backward.

- Fake a drive to the basket by making a jab step at your defender.
- Rock back to the triple-threat position.
- If the defender lunges forward, take a long step and drive.
- If the defender drops off, shoot the jump shot.

As a variation, you can add a shot fake after returning to the triple-threat position. If the defender goes for the fake, dribble drive to the basket.

Step-Back, One-Dribble Jump Shot

The step-back, one-dribble move is used to create space from your defender in order to shoot a jump shot.

- Make a jab step at your defender.
- When your defensive player retreats, take a step back behind your body with the jab-step foot.
- Dribble back with your dominant hand and move your pivot foot back into a balanced shooting position.
- Pick up the ball in front of the knee on your shooting side.
- Take the ball straight up and shoot a jump shot. Be careful not to fade on your shot.

TIPS FOR SUCCESS

1. Always be a triple-threat to shoot, pass, or dribble.
2. Read your defender's position—then make your move.
3. Attack your defender's weak side.
4. Make a fake look like the real thing.
5. Keep your knees bent on all shot fakes.
6. Fake in one direction and move in the other.
7. Use a crossover step when you are overplayed.
8. Anytime you get your foot even with the defender's foot, drive past the player.

Inside Moves

"It is important that your post man

touches the ball. Get him involved

even if his primary role is defense

or rebounding."

—John Thompson, Naismith Basketball
Hall of Fame coach

Every player, regardless of size, must learn how to score inside. Even perimeter players will have opportunities to score inside against defenders similar in size. Perfecting inside moves will help you become a complete offensive scorer.

The Importance of the Inside Game

Team success depends on the inside game. Most coaches build their offense from the inside out. Getting the ball inside helps in the following ways:

- It produces high-percentage shots.
- It increases the chances of being fouled by your opponent.
- It forces the defense to collapse, thus opening up three-point shooting opportunities.

Post-Up Stance

The first step in becoming an inside scorer is learning how to post up. The correct post-up stance keeps your defender out of the passing lane so that you can receive the pass. You must make contact with your opponent with your back, shoulder, and upper arm and keep him or her from the passing lane. Be prepared for physical contact in the post area. Key teaching points in the post-up stance are:

- Assume a floor position just outside the free throw lane and above the free throw block.
- Maintain a wide base with a low center of gravity. Your shoulders should be square so that the passer can see the numbers on your jersey.

Team success depends on establishing an inside game.

When posting up, maintain a wide base and keep the defender out of the passing lane.

- Keep your elbows out and parallel to the floor.
- Give a two-hand target with fingers spread and pointing upward.
- Make contact and keep the defender in place. A teaching cue to emphasize this point is to "sit on the defender's legs."
- Keep your defender on your back. Do not allow the defensive player to get a foot in front of your foot.
- Meet the pass and catch the ball with two hands.

Getting Open

It is your responsibility to get open so you can receive a pass. There are a number of ways to do this:

- Beat your defender down the floor.
- Make a "V" cut (fake in one direction and go in the opposite direction).
- Flash cut to the openings between defenders.
- Step across your defender's front foot in order to establish an open passing lane.
- Execute a reverse pivot to seal your defender from the passing lane. The best way to do this is to momentarily face your defender and place your foot in between his or her feet. Execute a reverse pivot and you will have your defender on your back.
- Backdoor cut when your defender completely fronts you.

Read the Defense and the Ball Handler

Reading the defense involves seeing your defender and/or feeling your defender's body against yours. Always focus your attention on the floor position of both the ball handler and your defensive player.

If you are located on the opposite side of the court from the ball, look to flash across the lane into an open area. Your objective is to cut in front of your defender so you have the inside position to receive a pass.

When you are on the same side of the court as the ball handler, position yourself on an imaginary line through the ball and the basket, as shown in Figure 11.1. This is called getting "on track" with the passer. It shortens the pass from the post feeder and provides the best passing angle.

Successful inside players always read their defenders in order to create scoring openings. The following guidelines will place you in position to score more effectively:

- If defended on the low side, take the defensive player a step or two lower and post up.
- If defended on the high side, take the defensive player a step or two higher and post up.
- If fronted, move closer to the ball, seal the defender, and look for the lob pass or ball reversal.
- If guarded from behind, establish contact, keep the defender in place, and post up.

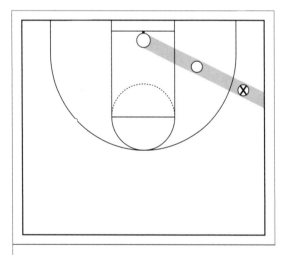

Figure 11.1 To pass the ball inside, the ball handler and the post-up player must get "on track."

Think One Pass Ahead

Another way to establish open passing lanes is to think one pass ahead. There are many times when a perimeter player cannot get the ball to you. Do not give up your post-up position or get discouraged. By maintaining contact with your defender, you often will create a passing lane from a different angle.

As shown in Figure 11.2, imagine that you are posting up above the free throw block and the ball handler is at the wing. Your defender is playing on the low side, preventing a pass from being thrown to you. You must think one pass ahead. Maintain contact and keep the defensive player on the low side. You have established a new passing lane and will be open when the ball is passed out front. Outstanding inside players are always thinking one pass ahead and establish new passing angles.

Catching the Pass

When receiving the ball from a post feeder, remember the following points:

- Reach for the pass.
- Catch the ball with two hands.
- Land using a jump stop.
- Bring the ball immediately to a position under your chin. A key teaching cue to emphasize this point is "chin it."
- Keep your elbows out for protection.
- Locate and read the defense.

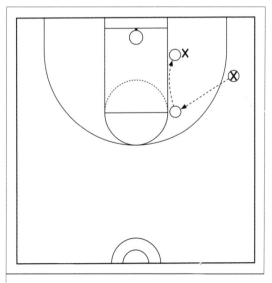

Figure 11.2 An inside player can create a new passing lane by maintaining contact and keeping the defender on the low side.

Inside Moves

There are several inside moves that you should perfect. Your choice will depend on the floor position of your defender and how far you are from the basket.

Drop Step

The drop step is used when the defensive player is positioned on the high side. The offensive player can execute the drop step with or without the dribble.

With the Dribble

- Pivot using a rear turn on the foot closest to the defender.
- Step toward the basket with the nonpivot foot.
- Seal off the defender with your body.
- Take one quick, low dribble, which should be kept between your legs so that the ball is not stolen. This dribble is called a crab dribble.
- Point your toes at the baseline.
- Take the ball up with two hands for protection.
- Do not open up and expose the ball to the defensive player.
- Shoot using the hand farthest from the defender.
- Use the backboard whenever possible.

Without the Dribble

- Execute the drop step before catching the pass, and do not dribble.
- Then follow the same moves as for the drop step with the dribble.

Jump Hook

The jump hook is used when the defender is playing on the low side. This is a very difficult shot for the defender to block, and, like the drop step, it can be used with or without a dribble.

With the Dribble

- Execute a rear-turn pivot with the baseline foot as the pivot foot.

Catch the ball with two hands and immediately "chin it."

- Use the nonpivot foot to step into the lane. Do not step away from the basket—this foot should point toward the sideline.
- Take one quick, low dribble.
- Point your shoulder at the basket.
- When your nonpivot foot hits the floor, swing the pivot foot into the lane. Your chest should be facing the sideline.
- Jump off both feet.
- Bring the ball up along the side of your head and release with full arm extension.
- Protect the ball with the nonshooting arm.

Without the Dribble

- Execute a rear-turn pivot with the baseline foot as the pivot foot.
- Step into the lane with the nonpivot foot—it serves as the takeoff foot for the shot.
- Raise your pivot foot and lift your knee high in the air.
- Bring the ball up along the side of your head and release with full arm extension.

Turnaround Jump Shot

The turnaround jump shot can be used when the defender is playing behind or on either side of the post player. The offensive player must create space from the defender in order to get the shot off.

- Catch the ball, chin it, and locate the defender.
- Pivot using a front turn on the foot farthest from your defender.
- Keep the ball above your chest during the pivot.
- Square up and take the jump shot.

When using the drop step, seal off the defender with your body.

Wheel-to-the-Middle Jump Hook

A combination of the drop step and the jump hook, the wheel-to-the-middle move is used when your defender cuts off the drop step. Good inside scorers always have countermoves when their initial moves are stopped by defenders.

- Maintain the same pivot foot during this move.
- Execute a drop step to the basket.
- If your defender slides over to stop the baseline move, pivot to the middle for a jump hook.

Up and Under

The up and under move is used to penetrate to the basket after the defensive player reacts to a shot fake.

- Pivot using a front turn and face the basket.
- Execute a shot fake. Keep your knees bent as you take the ball up on your shot fake.

When shooting the jump hook, protect the ball with the nonshooting arm and release the ball with full arm extension.

- If your defender goes up for the fake, step through quickly with the nonpivot foot.
- Bring the ball across your body with speed and quickness.
- Take a long, quick step toward the basket.
- Execute this move with or without a dribble.

TIPS FOR SUCCESS

1. Be prepared for physical contact.
2. Keep your hands up and always give a target.
3. Constantly work to get open.
4. Create contact to seal your defender.
5. Keep your defender on your back.
6. Reach out and meet the pass.
7. Chin the ball and read the defender.
8. Execute strong, quick moves to the basket.
9. Always protect the ball.
10. Use countermoves when your initial move is stopped.

Moving Without the Ball

"Perhaps the most important

part of offensive basketball is

the part played by each man

without the ball."

—John Wooden, Naismith Basketball
Hall of Fame coach

Since only one player at a time can handle the ball, theoretically you will be playing without the ball about 80 percent of the time. This statistic clearly illustrates the importance of developing skills that don't involve the ball.

Moving without the ball requires you to be adept at starting, stopping, faking, and changing directions. You must have excellent court awareness and vision so that you maintain the proper floor spacing with your teammates.

Many young players do not know how to move efficiently without the ball. They will either run directly toward the ball handler begging for a pass or stand in one place watching the ball handler dribble the ball. In *1980 Medalist Notebook*, NCAA champion coach Jim Valvano from North Carolina State said, "Offensive movement without the ball is one of the most important aspects of the game, and the least practiced."

Move with a Purpose

Remember your moves must have a purpose. Your movement should be coordinated with those of your teammates so that you are working as a smooth-functioning unit. You can move to an open area to receive a pass, you can set screens for teammates, or you can clear through to the other side of the court to create more room for the ball handler.

Moving without the ball requires skills in starting, stopping, faking, and changing direction.

Maintain Floor Balance

In *Basketball According to Knight and Newell*, Hall of Fame coaches Bob Knight and Pete Newell said, "There isn't anything that is more important than having our players distributed properly. We think, in all situations, the ideal spacing on the floor is 15 to 18 feet apart." Figure 12.1 shows this spacing.

Be careful not to bring your defender into an area that reduces the effectiveness of one of your teammates. It is impossible to maintain spacing at all times due to the many screens that are set. It is important, though, to always balance the floor after screening or cutting.

See the Ball and Your Defender Before Cutting

See the floor position of both the ball and your defensive player to determine when and where to move. There are three simple rules to follow:

1. When your defensive player is playing you high, take the player higher and then cut low.
2. When your defensive player is playing you low, take the player lower and cut high.
3. When your defensive player is in a sagging position, take the player close to the lane and then break out to a position where you can immediately take the shot.

Once you have decided your course of action, push off from the floor hard and move with quickness. Cuts should be sharp and made in a straight line. If you move in an arc, your defender can follow a straight path and beat you to the desired spot.

Figure 12.1 **Players on the perimeter must maintain proper floor balance and be 15–18 feet apart.**

Types of Cuts

You must be able to get open without the use of a screen. To accomplish this, you must become proficient in the following cuts.

"V" Cut

The "V" cut is a change-of-direction cut that takes the shape of the letter "V," as shown in Figure 12.2. It is designed to move your defender in a direction opposite from your intended cut.

- Move slowly into the "V" cut.
- Take your defender away from where you want to cut.
- Time your cut to coincide with when you want to receive the pass.

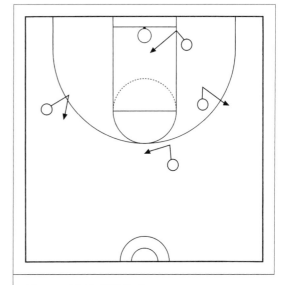

Figure 12.2 **"V" Cut**

- Take a three-quarter step with your outside foot and pivot in the direction you want to go. Push off hard and make a long second step past your defender.
- Get your hands up and be ready to receive a pass.

Back Cut

The back cut is a cut behind the defensive player and toward the basket. It is often used when your defender is overplaying and denying you the pass. Use the back cut whenever your defender's head is turned away from you.

Hall of Fame coach Pete Carril from Princeton University was considered one of the top coaches of all time in teaching players how to read a defense and how to react to it. He taught his players how to compete against players with superior athleticism and size. In his book *The Smart Take from the Strong*, Carril explained, "We have made a living out of the backdoor cut at Princeton. When you're guarded so closely that you aren't free to catch a pass, it means the defender is playing denial defense—he has turned his back partially to the ball. That's when you want to go backdoor. The defender can't watch the ball out front and you cutting behind him at the same time. We like to throw bounce passes off the dribble on our backdoor plays."

The back cut, shown in Figure 12.3, can be executed in one of two ways:

1. You can push off the outside foot and take a long step with the other leg.
2. You can pivot on the inside foot and execute a long crossover step toward the basket.

In either case, never lose sight of the ball and always give a hand target for the passer.

"L" Cut

Shown in Figure 12.4, the "L" cut is a change-of-direction cut that takes the shape of the letter "L." Use it when your defender is in the passing lane but is playing loosely.

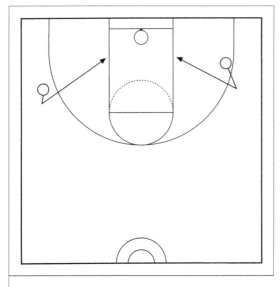

Figure 12.3 Back Cut

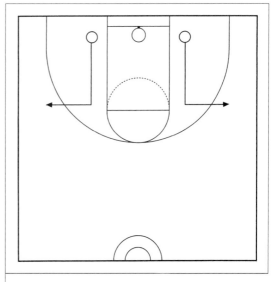

Figure 12.4 "L" Cut

- Move toward your defender; then push off hard and cut to the wing.
- This cut is effective because the offensive player closes the distance, making it difficult for the defender to react to the hard cut.

Inside Cut

An inside cut is used when the offensive player passes the ball to a teammate and cuts to the basket looking for a return pass. This maneuver is sometimes referred to as the "give and go."

The "give-and-go" style was introduced to the game of basketball in 1925 by the "Original Celtics" of New York City. For many years they were the professional champions of the world. Hall of Fame players "Dutch" Dehnert and Nat Holman perfected this play, and the "give-and-go" style highly influenced the progress of offensive basketball.

Today, every team offense uses inside cuts. The following are key points when executing the inside cut, diagrammed in Figure 12.5:

- After passing to a teammate, read your defender. If the player moves in the direction of the pass, use a "V" cut to set up your defender. If the defensive player stays stationary after your pass, it will not be necessary to use a "V" cut.

- Make a hard cut in front of your defender, creating an open passing lane.
- Get your hands up and be ready to receive a pass.

Shallow Cut

The shallow cut is a change-of-direction cut that is sometimes called a "fishhook" cut. Shown in Figure 12.6, it is used as a pressure release when you are being overplayed and the ball handler is dribbling toward you. The shallow cut is a very effective pressure release tactic because it forces your defender out of the denial position.

- If you are overplayed when a teammate is dribbling toward you, take several steps toward the basket and then move toward the dribbler.
- Make a quick "hook" back toward the ball for a pass from the ball handler.

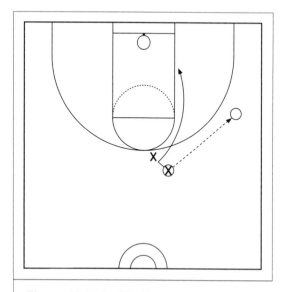

Figure 12.5 Inside Cut

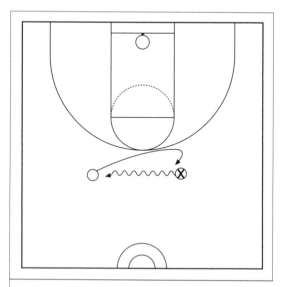

Figure 12.6 Shallow Cut

Clock-Down Cut

The clock-down cut is a cut toward the baseline by a help-side forward, shown in Figure 12.7. It is used to create an open passing lane for a crosscourt pass from a dribbler to an open shooter. This cut is a very effective strategy to create an open perimeter shot because your defender will normally leave you to help stop the drive to the basket.

When you are positioned on the wing opposite the ball and you see the ball handler drive to the basket:

- Make a cut toward the baseline.
- Go as close to the baseline as necessary to create an open passing lane.
- Have your hands up and anticipate the pass.

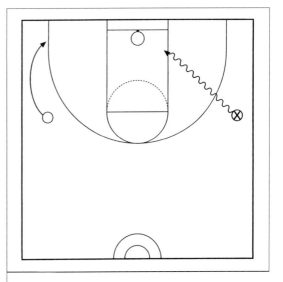

Figure 12.7 **Clock-Down Cut**

TIPS FOR SUCCESS

1. Maintain proper spacing (15–18 feet) from your teammates.
2. Always move with a purpose.
3. Read your defender before cutting.
4. Take your defender away from where you want to cut.
5. Time your cut.
6. Cut in a straight line.
7. Always have your hands up and anticipate the pass.

Screening

"Screening is the backbone of

modern basketball."

—Frank McGuire, Naismith Basketball
Hall of Fame coach

Screening is the offensive strategy of positioning a player in the path of a defender. It is the best way to help a teammate get open. Screens may be set for a player with or without the ball.

Effective screening places the defense at a tremendous disadvantage because it is difficult to stay with an offensive player coming off a good screen. If the defensive players switch, there is often a mismatch in height or ability. A defensive switch also creates inside positioning for the screener to receive a pass.

Setting a Screen
As a screener, it is your responsibility to get the cutter open for a pass or shot. Dr. Jerry Krause from Gonzaga University used the teaching cue "loud, low, and legal" to describe how a player should set a screen.

The following are key teaching points when setting a screen off the ball:

1. **Assume a wide stance.**
   - Come to a jump stop with the feet shoulder-width apart.
   - Place your hands in front of your midsection, both for protection and as a reminder not to overextend, grab, or push the defender.

2. **Establish the proper angle.**
   - Set the screen perpendicular to the expected path of the defender.
   - Your back should be square to the area where the cutter will receive the pass.
   - Set the screen approximately an arm's-length away from the defender.

3. **Hold the screen.**
   - Be firmly set.
   - Be ready for contact.

4. **React to the defender and the cutter.**
   - When the defender attempts to fight through the screen, your teammate using the screen is usually open.
   - When the defenders switch, the screener will be open.

5. **"Shape up" after the screen.**
   - After setting the screen, turn toward the ball.
   - Get your hands up and be ready to receive the pass.

The best way to help a teammate get open is by setting a screen.

Receiving the Screen

When a teammate screens for you, it is your responsibility to drive your defender into the screen. Here are the key teaching points when using an off-the-ball screen:

1. **Set up your defender.**
   - Use a "V" cut, as shown in Figure 13.1, so that you take your defender in a direction opposite that of your intended cut.

2. **Wait for the screen.**
   - Be patient. It is better to be a second late than to break too early.
   - Give the screener time to get set.

3. **Cut directly off the screen.**
   - Drive your defender into the screen.
   - Make shoulder contact with the screener as you cut.

4. **Read the defense.**
   - Read your defender.
   - Match the type of cut you make to the floor position of your defensive player.

5. **Be ready for the pass.**
   - Get your hands up as you come off the screen.

Types of Screens

The floor position of your teammate's defender determines the type of screen you will set. The following are off-the-ball screens:

- **Down Screen.** The down screen, diagrammed in Figure 13.2, is used when an offensive player moves toward the baseline to free an offensive cutter on the perimeter.

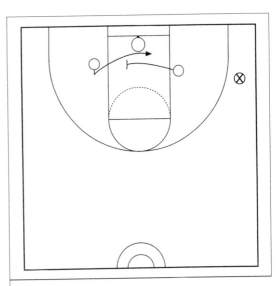

Figure 13.1 When receiving a screen, wait for the screen to be set and make a "V" cut prior to using the screen.

- **Cross Screen.**
  The cross screen is
  used when an
  offensive player
  moves laterally to
  set a screen for a
  teammate in the
  post area. See
  Figure 13.3.

- **Back Screen.** The
  back screen is
  used when an
  offensive player
  moves away from
  the basket to set a
  screen. As shown

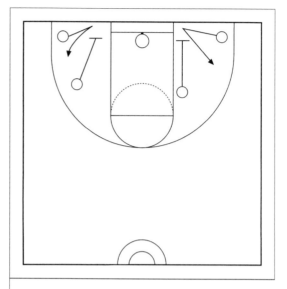

Figure 13.2 **Down Screen**

in Figure 13.4, the cutter breaks either over the top or underneath the
screen toward the basket. The back screen is used against defenders
who are overplaying.

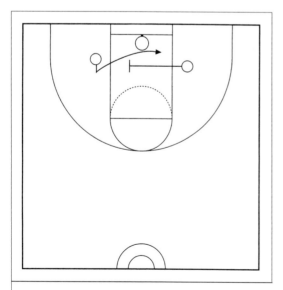

Figure 13.3 **Cross Screen**

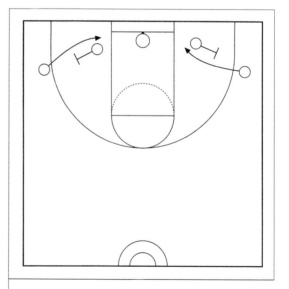

Figure 13.4 **Back Screen**

Cutting Off the Screen

It is the responsibility of the player using the screen to cut off the screen at the right time and move to the right place. You must recognize the floor position of your defender in order to make the most productive cut.

The following are examples of different types of cuts that can be made from off-the-ball screens:

1. **Wing Cut.** If your defender is playing tight defense, drive the player into the screen and make a hard cut to the perimeter, depicted in Figure 13.5.

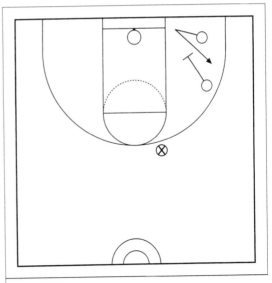

Figure 13.5 **Wing Cut**

2. **Fade Cut.** If your defender is playing high and there is distance between you and the defensive player, cut away from the player to create additional space. See Figure 13.6.

3. **Curl Cut.** If your defender is trailing you, curl sharply off the screen toward the basket as shown in Figure 13.7.

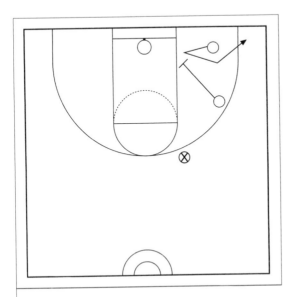

Figure 13.6 **Fade Cut**

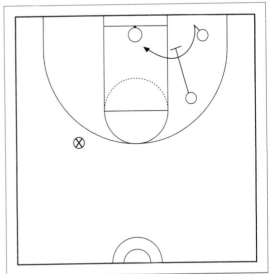

Figure 13.7 **Curl Cut**

4. **Back Cut.** If your defender beats you over the screen, execute a back cut toward the basket, as diagrammed in Figure 13.8. Never lose sight of the ball. Remember to push off hard from the floor and present a target for the ball handler.

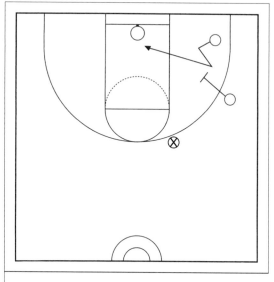

Figure 13.8 Back Cut

Pick-and-Roll (Screen and Roll)

Pick-and-roll is an offensive term used to describe a screen on the ball handler's defender. It is the most frequently used play in the NBA. When properly executed, the pick-and-roll is extremely difficult to defend and often creates mismatches in height or speed against teams that switch.

It takes timing, proper footwork, nonverbal communication, and experience to perfect the pick-and-roll. John Stockton and Karl Malone were the best in the NBA and made the pick-and-roll the trademark of the Utah Jazz.

The following are key teaching points for the basic pick-and-roll play:

When Setting the Screen

- Use a two-footed jump stop and assume a wide stance.
- Keep your arms in to avoid an illegal moving screen.
- Roll to the basket by pivoting on the inside foot.
- Swing the arm and shoulder as you roll in order to accelerate the turning action.
- Put a target hand in the air.
- Never lose sight of the ball.

- Set up your defender by moving or faking in a direction opposite that of the screen.
- Rub shoulders with the screener as you use the screen.
- Use two dribbles to go past the screen and create space for the pass to the screener rolling to the basket.
- Keep your head up and read the defense.

Reading the Defense

The success of the screen on the ball depends on the ability of the screener and the ball handler to read the defense.

- **When the defenders switch.** As shown in Figure 13.9, when defensive players X1 and X5 switch on the screen, O1 takes two dribbles past the screen and looks to pass to O5 rolling to the basket. Note that O5 has inside position against the smaller defensive guard X1. This action is called the pick-and-roll and is used to combat the defensive switch.
- **When the defender attempts to fight over the screen.** As shown in Figure 13.10, when X1 attempts to stay with O1 and fight over the screen, O1 looks to turn the corner and drive to the basket for either a layup or an open jump shot.
- **When the defender goes below the screen.** When X1 goes below O5's screen and X5, as shown in

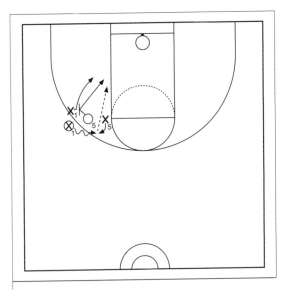

Figure 13.9 **When the defenders switch**

Figure 13.11, this creates space for O1 to use the screen and pull up for an open jump shot.

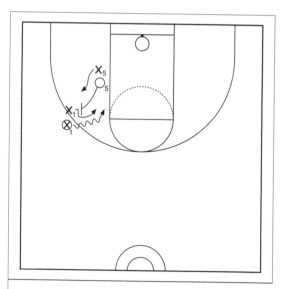

Figure 13.10 When the defender attempts to fight over the screen

- **When the screener's defender steps out early.** As shown in Figure 13.12, when X5 steps out early in an attempt to slow down the dribbler O1, O5 releases early and makes a direct cut to the basket. O1 passes to O5 cutting toward the basket.

- **When the screener's defender drops back.** As you can see in Figure 13.13, when X5 drops back to allow X1 to slide through O5's screen, O5

Figure 13.11 **When the defender goes below the screen**

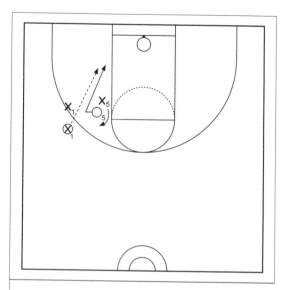

Figure 13.12 **When the screener's defender steps out early**

"pops" to the wing and looks for an open shot. This action is called the pick-and-pop.

● **When the defenders trap the ball handler.** When both defenders X1 and X5 trap the ball handler, O1 uses a pull-back dribble to create space and pass to O5, as shown in Figure 13.14. This creates an offensive advantage because the defense will be outnumbered.

Figure 13.13 When the screener's defender drops back

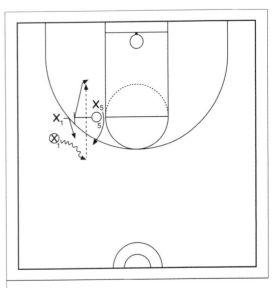

Figure 13.14 When the defenders trap the ball handler

TIPS FOR SUCCESS

For the Screener

1. Set a low, legal screen.
2. Establish the proper angle.
3. Hold the screen.
4. "Shape up," or roll, after setting the screen.

For the Player Using the Screen

1. Wait for the screen.
2. Set up your defender.
3. Go shoulder-to-shoulder off the screen.
4. Read the defense.
5. Look for a scoring opportunity.

Offensive Rebounding

"Offensive rebounding demoralizes
your opponent and is the best way
for your team to get more shots."

—Bailey Howell, Naismith Basketball
Hall of Fame player

The importance of offensive rebounding cannot be overemphasized. Even when your team shoots well, it is difficult to win if you only get one shot. Attacking the offensive boards produces high-percentage shots, more free throws, and a distinct psychological advantage over the defense.

The key to securing an offensive rebound is being at the right place at the right time. The period of time between the release of the shot and the point when the ball can be rebounded is crucial. During these few seconds a player must determine the distance and angle of the rebound and secure inside rebounding position.

Tynes Hildebrand, former coach at Northwestern State University, annually produced outstanding offensive rebounding teams. Besides teaching the correct techniques, Hildebrand made offensive rebounding a part of every drill during practice and designated an assistant coach to focus on offensive rebounding at all times.

Offensive rebounding is a key factor in winning basketball games.

Qualities of Outstanding Offensive Rebounders

Offensive rebounding is a state of mind. To become an outstanding rebounder, you should have the following qualities:

1. **Anticipation**
   - Assume that every shot will be missed.
   - Know the location of the shot and the distance from the basket.
   - The timing of your jump is more important than the height.

2. **Determination**
   - Rebounding is 75 percent desire and 25 percent ability.
   - Refuse to be blocked out by a defender.

3. **Hustle**
   - Get the inside rebounding position.
   - Make the second and third effort.
   - Be aggressive.

Play every shot as if it will be a missed shot.

Rebound Location

As the shot is taken, you should make every effort to be in a position to rebound a missed shot. The location of a rebound depends on three factors:

1. **The Distance of the Shot from the Basket**
   - Normally the longer the shot, the longer the rebound.
   - Do not position yourself under the basket because the only ball that you will be able to secure is one that has gone through the hoop.

2. **The Angle of the Shot**
   - A missed shot from the wing or corner will be rebounded on the help side approximately 70 percent of the time.
   - A missed shot from the middle of the floor is more difficult to gauge.

3. **The Shooter's Touch**
   - A shot with high arc and backspin will have less of a rebound.
   - A shot with low arc and sidespin will rebound farther from the basket.

In *Bird on Basketball*, legendary player Larry Bird compared offensive rebounding to picking apples. "The basket is an apple tree. Rebounds are its apples. Your defensive man is a fence around the tree. You want the apples, but you either have to wait for them to fall on your side of the fence, or carefully jump up and grab them without getting hurt on your fence. The only other way you can pick the apples is to find a hole in the fence somewhere and squeeze through, but that's hard to do."

Your first priority is to secure the inside rebound position. If you can't establish the inside spot, get even or alongside your defensive player so you have an equal chance for the rebound. Even if you can't get the rebound, always try to get a hand on the ball and keep it alive. By doing this, you may help one of your teammates get the rebound.

Another option is to block in the defender who gets too far under the basket. This will neutralize that player's inside position advantage because the rebound will travel over his or her head.

Be aggressive and attempt to secure the inside rebound position.

If you are the shooter, follow your shot as soon as you complete the follow-through. You should have a better idea of where the ball will go than anyone else on the court.

Offensive Rebounding Rules

Adhering to the following rules will help you become an excellent offensive rebounder:

- Assume every shot will be missed.
- Be aggressive and want the ball.
- Do not watch the flight of the ball.
- Anticipate the location of the rebound.
- Move to that spot and secure the inside position.
- Keep your hands up in a ready position.
- Do not allow the defensive player to block.

Footwork to Counter the Block-Out

You are at a distinct disadvantage as an offensive rebounder because the defensive players are closer to the basket. The following techniques will help you gain inside rebounding position:

1. **Step in Front**
   - Use this technique when the defender is watching the flight of the ball and not trying to block out.
   - Quickly step in front of the defender and establish inside position.
2. **Arm over, Step over**
   - When the defender is attempting to block out, use your upper arm to push down the opponent's arm.
   - At the same time, quickly step in front and block out the defender.
3. **Crossover Step**
   - Use this technique when your defender moves too far sideways in an attempt to block out.
   - Make a fake in one direction and use a crossover step to move past the defender.

4. **Rear Turn and Spin**
    - Use this maneuver when your defender has established contact and is between you and the basket.
    - Place one foot between your defender's legs and execute a rear pivot.
    - Spin off the defender with your hands up.

Take the Ball to the Basket

An offensive rebound should be thought of as a pass to the basket. After securing an offensive rebound, take the ball to the basket and finish the play. To score after an offensive rebound:

- Land with good balance.
- Make a strong power move toward the basket.
- Use head and shot fakes, if necessary.
- Concentrate on the basket.
- Expect contact.
- Protect the ball.
- Use the backboard if possible.
- Be quick without hurrying.

After securing an offensive rebound, take the ball to the basket and finish the play.

TIPS FOR SUCCESS

1. Assume all shots will be missed.
2. Be active and do not watch the flight of the ball.
3. Determine the distance and angle of the rebound.
4. Gain inside position.
5. Get your hands up in a ready position.
6. Be aggressive and go after the missed shot.
7. Make the second and third effort.
8. After securing the rebound, take the ball to the basket and finish the play.

Offensive
Drills

"If there were a secret in

successful basketball, then

that secret would be drilling

on fundamentals."

—Adolph Rupp, Naismith
Basketball Hall of Fame coach

Shooting Drills for Younger Players

> "A minimum of 30 minutes each
>
> practice should be devoted to
>
> shooting."
>
> —Bill Sharman, Naismith Basketball
> Hall of Fame player

The main purpose of basketball programs in the elementary grades should be to create interest in the game, promote teamwork and fair play, and develop basic skills. It is essential to teach young players the correct shooting mechanics. But it is difficult for players to demonstrate the correct fundamentals using a regulation-size ball and a 10-foot basket. One way to help young players develop good shooting habits is to use a smaller ball and lower the rim.

Another common practice that leads to incorrect shooting habits is long-range shooting. Many young players like to shoot from a distance outside of their range, and they are forced to deviate from proper shooting alignment.

The basic shooting fundamentals and alignment are the same for all perimeter shots and should be taught to players at an early age.

Steps for Shooting Success for Beginning Players

To develop perimeter shooting skills, a beginning player must be taught:

- The importance of balance and footwork
- The proper grip for the shooting hand and the balance hand
- How to align the hand, wrist, and elbow
- How to square up to the basket and be in the proper alignment
- The proper shooting rhythm and follow-through

Key Shooting Fundamentals for Younger Players

Shooting fundamentals change as young players mature.

Elementary School Players

The shooting distance from the basket should be anywhere from 5 to 15 feet, depending on the strength and development of the player.

- Point your feet at the basket, shoulder-width apart with the shooting foot slightly ahead.
- Square your body to the basket.
- Place your shooting hand and balance hand on the ball in the correct positions.
- Start with the ball in your shooting pocket with your fingers positioned upward. This will place the arm in the low elbow lift position as shown in Photo 15.1. This position makes it easier for you to control the shot.
- Bend your knees and "load the gun" by cocking your wrist so that the ball is below your forehead. The index finger of your shooting hand should be in line with the outside part of your cheek.

- Thrust the ball up and forward.
- Hold your follow-through.
- After grooving your shot from a stationary position, begin to use a slight jump.

Middle School Players

The shooting distance from the basket should be anywhere from 5 to 18 feet, depending on the strength and development of the player.

***Photo 15.1* Low Elbow Lift Position**

- Continue practicing the core fundamentals of shooting (BEEF, as described in Chapter 5).
- Begin to use a low jump or a slight hop to initiate your shot.
- As you improve your shooting fundamentals, look to raise your elbow to a position that it is even with the shoulder. This is called the medium elbow lift position and is shown in Photo 15.2. Use a medium jump to initiate the shot.

Shooting Drills for Beginning Players

A number of drills will help beginning players improve their shot.

Load the Gun

- Face the basket with the feet shoulder-width apart and the shooting foot slightly ahead.
- Hold the ball in the shooting pocket with the fingers pointed upward.
- Check the placement of your shooting hand and the balance hand.

***Photo 15.2* Medium Elbow Lift Position**

- On the command "Ready," lock the wrist and cock it back. As shown in Photo 15.3, the back of the hand should be approximately parallel with the floor.
- Hold this position and check the alignment of your feet, hand, wrist, and elbow.

Catch and Load the Gun

- Receive a pass from a partner and quickly adjust your grip as you "load the gun."
- Pass the ball back to your partner. Continue for 10 consecutive passes.
- If you do not have a partner, place the ball on the floor. Quickly pick up the ball and adjust your grip as you "load the gun."

Photo 15.3 **Load the Gun Position**

Shoot for the Stars

- As shown in Photo 15.4, lie down on your back with the ball in the shooting pocket.
- Check the placement of your shooting hand and the balance hand.
- Check the alignment of your hand, wrist, and elbow.
- Cock your wrist and thrust the ball up and forward.
- Extend the shooting arm into the air and hold the follow-through.
- Aim to have the ball return to the starting position without having to move your hands.

Photo 15.4 **Shoot for the Stars Drill**

- Your goal is to shoot five consecutive shots that return straight back to your hands.
- Work to gradually increase the height of the shot.

Form Shots

- Face an imaginary basket with your feet shoulder-width apart and the shooting foot slightly ahead. Using the proper shooting techniques, shoot the ball so that it lands slightly in front of you.
- Slightly flex your knees and waist.
- Balance the ball in your shooting pocket with the fingers pointing upward.
- Check the placement of your shooting hand and balance hand.
- "Load the gun" and bring the ball straight up past the face.
- Keep your elbow up and under the ball.
- Thrust the ball up and forward with the fingers.
- Release the ball off your fingertips.
- Hold the follow-through until the ball hits the floor.
- Catch the ball off the bounce and continue shooting.

Nothing but Net

- Stand approximately 3 feet in front of the basket.
- Using all the correct fundamentals of shooting, attempt to make the basket hitting only net.
- After making five consecutive shots that hit nothing but net, move back one step.
- Continue to move back after you have made five consecutive shots.

Bank Shots

- The Bank Shots drill is the same as the Nothing But Net drill, except that you shoot from a 45-degree angle on each side of the basket.
- Position yourself approximately 4 feet from the basket.
- Aim for the upper corner of the backboard rectangle.
- After making five consecutive shots, move to the other side.
- Continue the drill by moving back one step.

Square Up to the Basket

- The purpose of this drill is to help maintain your balance as you square up to the basket prior to your shot.
- Hold a basketball in your shooting pocket.
- Check the position of your shooting hand and balance hand.
- Jog in a circular pattern. If you are practicing on a court, jog around the center circle.
- A partner or coach will suddenly point to a basket. It could be either of the baskets on the main court, or it could be a basket on a side court.
- Quickly react to your partner's command by coming to a quick stop with your toes pointing toward the designated basket. Square your shoulders and "load the gun" as if you were going to shoot the basketball.
- After 30 seconds, change direction.
- The next progression of this drill is to shoot the ball to yourself, just like you did in the Form Shots drill. Hold your follow-through until the ball hits the floor. Catch the ball off the bounce and continue your movement around the circle until your partner points to another basket.

Overhand Layup Drills for Beginning Players

The layup shot is a challenging skill for beginning players because it combines the skills of dribbling and shooting. It takes excellent footwork and balance to become proficient in layup shooting. An additional challenge is learning how to use the nondominant hand when shooting a layup.

The most common layup shooting errors for beginning players are (1) taking your eyes off the target; (2) taking off too soon; (3) taking off too late; and (4) taking off on the wrong foot.

The best way to teach young players how to shoot a layup is to use the part-whole method. The following drills are highly recommended.

Step and High Jump

- Position yourself two steps away from the basket at a 45-degree angle from the backboard.
- Hold an imaginary ball.

- Take a short step with the foot opposite from the hand that would be shooting if you had a ball. Drive the other leg and knee up and toward the basket.
- Keep your head up and eyes focused on the top corner of the backboard square.

Step and Shoot

- Hold a ball in your hands and position yourself just like you did for the Step and High Jump drill.
- Position your shooting hand in the center and on the back of the ball.
- Position your balance hand on the side of the ball.
- Take a short step with the foot opposite the shooting hand. Drive the other leg and knee up and toward the basket.
- Keep your eyes focused on the target.
- Extend the elbow and flex your wrist and fingers forward.
- Keep the balance hand on the ball until the release.
- Shoot the ball softly off the top corner of the backboard square.
- See the ball go through the net.

Dribble and Shoot

- Start three steps away from the basket.
- Take a step with the foot on the same side as your shooting hand.
- Dribble once and bring the nondribbling hand to the ball as you jump off the foot opposite from the shooting hand.
- Drive the shooting leg and knee up and toward the basket.
- Extend the elbow and flex your wrist and fingers forward.
- Shoot the ball high and soft off the top corner of the backboard square.

Shooting Drills

"Fundamentals are the basis for

excellence. The player who can

feint an opponent out of position in

a game, drive to the basket, and

make a successful shot acquired

all of these abilities through

practice."

—Clair Bee, Naismith Basketball
Hall of Fame coach

Players spend the majority of their free time practicing shooting. Unfortunately, most players do not spend this time in a productive manner because they do not simulate game conditions or reinforce the correct shooting techniques. As you practice shooting, always remember: *Take game shots, at game spots, at game speed.*

Individual Shooting Drills

1. **Ball Slap.** The first drill is to simply grip the ball in both hands with the fingers evenly spread. Slap the ball hard with one hand and then the other. Do this 15–20 times. This drill develops the proper spread of the fingers and strengthens your grip.

2. **Form Shots.** Face an imaginary basket with your feet shoulder-width apart and the shooting foot slightly ahead. Using the proper shooting techniques, shoot the ball so that it lands slightly in front of you. Do this 5–10 times.

3. **Nothing but Net.** Start 5 feet from the basket and attempt to hit nothing but net as you shoot. After making three shots in a row, gradually work your way out to the free throw line.

4. **Bank Shots.** Position yourself approximately 4 feet from the basket. Aim for the upper corner of the backboard rectangle. Make three shots in a row from both sides of the floor.

5. **Shoot off the Pass.** Flip the ball out, receive it off the bounce, and take a perimeter shot. Start approximately 10 feet from the basket and gradually work your way out to your maximum shooting range. This drill helps develop your footwork and your ability to square up to the basket.

6. **Shoot off the Dribble.** This drill develops your shooting footwork off the dribble. Use both the direct drive and the crossover step. Start approximately 10 feet from the basket and gradually work out to your maximum shooting range.

7. **Three in a Row.** Shoot at one spot and do not move to another spot until you make three shots in a row. Always practice shots that you will use in a game. Practice shots off the dribble and from a pass. Add shot fakes prior to shooting.

Partner Shooting Drills

1. **Ten Shots.** One player is the shooter for 10 consecutive shots while the other player is the rebounder and passer. The shooter moves to various spots on the floor after every shot. Always take game shots and stay within your shooting range. The players exchange positions after 10 shots. As a variation, shoot off the dribble and use shot fakes.

2. **Shoot Until You Miss.** One player shoots from a designated spot on the floor; the other player is the rebounder and passer. Continue to shoot until you miss and then exchange positions with the other player.

3. **Cut and Shoot.** One player shoots coming off an imaginary screen; the other player is the passer. Use different cuts coming off the imaginary screen (wing cut, fade cut, curl cut, and back cut). Follow your shot, put back any misses, and then make a pass to your partner who is cutting off an imaginary screen. Continue until each player has shot 10 shots.

Three-Player Shooting Drills

1. **Two-Ball Shooting.** Three players and two balls are needed for this drill. Designate two shooting spots approximately 12–15 feet apart. The players set up as either a shooter, a passer, or a rebounder. To begin the drill the shooter and the passer each have a ball. The shooter attempts a shot, moves to the other shooting spot, and receives a pass from the passer. The rebounder retrieves every shot and throws the ball to the passer. The shooter continues to move between the two designated spots and attempts 10 shots. The shooter keeps track of the number of made field goals. After 10 shots, the players change positions.

2. **Shoot Under Pressure.** This drill utilizes three players and one ball. One player is under the basket with the ball while the other two players form a single-file line at a designated shooting spot. The player positioned under the basket begins the drill by throwing a pass to the first player in line who becomes the shooter. The passer rushes at the shooter with his or her hand up but does not block the shot. The shooter must maintain concentration and shoot over the outstretched hand. The shooter rebounds the shot, passes the ball to the next shooter, and rushes out with a hand extended. The passer returns to the line after the shooter has taken a shot. After each player has attempted five shots, move to another shooting spot.

Shooting Games

1. **Beat Michael Jordan.** In this drill you are attempting to beat an imaginary Michael Jordan. Begin the game with a free throw. If you make the

shot, you receive one point. If you miss the free throw, Jordan gets three points. Now shoot field goals from a designated spot; score one point for yourself if you make the shot and two points for Jordan if you miss. The game is played to 11 points.

2. **Game-Winning Free Throws.** In this individual shooting drill, imagine that time has expired and you are shooting a one-and-one free throw. Your team is trailing by one point. You must make two free throws to win the game. If you shoot and miss the first attempt, run the length of the court four times. If you make the first shot but miss the second, run the length of the court two times.

3. **25 in a Row.** This is an individual shooting drill and is a great warm-up. It is a variation of a shooting drill used by legendary Hall of Fame coach Forrest "Phog" Allen from the University of Kansas. You must make 25 consecutive shots from five spots close to the basket. The shooting spots are: 3 feet directly in front of the basket; 1 foot inside the block on both the right side and left side; and 1 foot outside the block on both the right side and left side. Move from one spot to the next until you make 25 consecutive shots. Anytime you miss a shot, go back to the first spot in front of the basket. The number of consecutive shots can be modified depending on a player's age and talent level.

4. **Free Throws to 10.** This drill can be played with any number of players. Each player shoots one free throw at a time. Award two points for a made shot that hits only net and one point for a made shot that touches the rim. Deduct two points for a missed shot. The first player to get 10 points is the winner.

5. **"21."** Players take turns shooting a perimeter shot followed by a layup. Two points are awarded for a successful perimeter shot and one point for a layup. During each turn a player will attempt one perimeter shot and one layup shot. The first player to reach 21 is the winner. However, the game must end on a perimeter shot. This means that after reaching 19 or 20 points, you must make a long shot to win the game.

6. **"33."** Players take turns attempting three-pointers from various spots on the floor. A made basket is worth three points. The first player to score 33 points (11 baskets) is the winner.

7. **Around the World.** This game can be played with several players. Each player must wait until it is his or her turn to shoot. There are five

shooting spots: right corner, right wing, top of the circle, left wing, and left corner. The game begins with players shooting from the right corner. You must make the shot before moving to the next shooting spot, which in this case is the right wing. If you miss the shot, you may stay and wait for your next turn, or you can "chance it" and shoot again. However, if you "chance it" and miss the second attempt, you must return back to the shooting spot where you started the game. The winner is the first player to get to the opposite corner and then back to the corner where the game started.

8. **Horse.** This game can be played with any number of players. The first player starts the game and attempts a shot. If the shot is made, the second player must shoot the same type of shot from the same location. If the shot is missed, the second player receives the letter *H*. If the shot is made, the third player in line must attempt the same shot. After a shot is missed, it is the next player's turn to select the type of shot. Players who receive the letters *H*, *O*, *R*, *S*, and *E* are eliminated from the game.

9. **Knockout.** At least five players are needed for this game. Form a single-file line at a designated shooting spot; the first two players in line have balls. The first player takes a perimeter shot and, if necessary, rebounds the ball and tries to score as quickly as possible. The object of the game is to make a basket before the player behind you scores, or you are out of the game. The second player can shoot as soon as the ball leaves the first player's hand. If you make the shot, quickly pass the ball back to the next player. The game continues until there is only one player.

10. **Seven-Up.** At least four players are needed for this game. The players form a single-file line at a designated shooting spot. The first player attempts a perimeter shot. If the shot is made, the second player must make the shot or receives one point. In Seven-Up, you do not want to receive points. If the second player also makes the shot, the third player must hit the shot or is given two points. In other words, whenever you miss a shot, you receive the same number of points as the number of field goals that were made in a row prior to your miss. You are out of the game once you have accumulated seven points. The last player in the game is the winner.

11. **Offensive Rebounding–Perimeter Shooting Game.** This game is played with two players. One player takes seven perimeter shots from designated spots. The other player attempts to tip in any missed shot. If the shooter makes the perimeter shot, it is worth one point. If the rebounder tips in the missed shot, it is worth two points. After seven shots, the players exchange positions. The first player to earn 21 points is the winner.

12. **Seven Then Three in a Row.** Divide the players into two teams. One team shoots from the right elbow and the other team shoots from the left elbow. The first player shoots, retrieves the ball, and passes to the next player in line. Each basket counts one point for the team. For a team to win, the team must make seven baskets and then hit three shots in a row.

Quickness and Agility Drills

"We are extremely demanding in practice. We emphasize quickness, concentration, and mental toughness every day."

—Jack Greynolds, high school champion coach

Quickness is an essential ingredient for success in basketball. Players make split-second decisions and are continually starting, stopping, changing directions, and changing speeds. Outstanding players are able to think quickly as well as move their feet and hands quickly. The following drills will help you in these areas.

Foot Quickness

1. **Speed Rope Jumping.** Jump as quickly as you can for 60 seconds. Take a 30-second rest and then jump again. Do a total of three sets. Keep track of the number of jumps you make for each set. As a variation, do backward jumping and move the rope over your head from front to back.

2. **Line Rope Jumping—Front and Back.** Position yourself behind a line on the floor. Jump over the line going forward and backward as you perform your rope jumping. Do not step on the line. Record the number of jumps you make in 60 seconds.

3. **Line Rope Jumping—Side to Side.** Place your feet parallel to the line. Jump over the line by going from side to side for 60 seconds and record the number of jumps you make.

4. **Square Rope Jumping.** Jump in the shape of a square as you do your rope jumping. Perform one set for 60 seconds. Change direction and do another set for 60 seconds.

5. **Alternate-Feet Rope Jumping.** Jump as quickly as you can for 60 seconds by jumping twice on your left foot and then twice on your right foot. Perform two sets using a 30-second rest interval.

6. **Rope Jumping—Three Jumps and a Double Jump.** Jump three times and then do a double jump. The rope will go around twice before your feet touch the floor. Do two sets using a 60-second work period and a 30-second rest interval.

7. **Rope Jumping—Three Jumps and an Arm Cross.** Jump three times and then quickly cross your arms as the rope comes over your head. Continue with three more jumps and then do another arm cross. Do two sets using a 60-second work period and a 30-second rest interval.

Hand Quickness

1. **Ball-Hip-Ball.** Bend your knees and hold the ball with two hands in front of your waist. Drop the ball, quickly touch your hips with your hands, and grab the ball before it hits the floor. Continue the drill for 30 seconds. If you have a partner, have that player put his or her hand on top of the ball at the beginning of the drill. After you drop the ball, your partner's hand

will stay at that height. This keeps you from throwing the ball up in the air higher than your waist.

2. **Ball-Shoulder-Ball.** This drill is similar to Ball-Hip-Ball except now you will touch your shoulders rather than your hips. Grab the ball before it hits the ground and continue this action for 30 seconds.

3. **Ball-Shoulder-Hip-Ball.** This is a more advanced drill and requires you to touch both your shoulders and your hips after you drop the ball. Move your hands in a circular motion as you touch both your shoulders and hips. Grab the ball before it touches the floor and continue the drill for 30 seconds.

4. **Ball-Hip-Shoulder-Ball.** This is the most difficult of the hand quickness drills. After dropping the ball, you must touch your hips first and then your shoulders. Quickly grab the ball before it touches the floor.

Basketball Quickness Circuit

At Alma College and Limestone College, my staff and I developed a basketball quickness circuit that really improved our players' quickness and conditioning. Our players named the circuit "Death Row" or "The Dirty Dozen."

We varied the work interval from 30 seconds to 45 seconds. We allowed a 15-second rest interval as the players moved quickly from one station to the next. Our players went through the circuit twice.

1. **Slalom.** Place tape on the floor in the shape of the letter "V." The width at the top of the "V" should be 3–4 feet. Start at the base and jump from side to side with your feet together. Always land outside the tape. Jump forward to the top of the "V" and then jump backward to the base of the letter. Always jump with your hands up in a ready position, at about shoulder height.

2. **"U" Jump.** Place tape on the floor in the shape of a cross. Start in the upper right-hand corner. Jump down, across, and up without touching a line. From the upper left-hand corner, jump down, across, and up. You are jumping in the shape of the letter "U." Keep your hands about shoulder height as you jump.

3. **Heel Clicks.** Place two parallel strips of tape 1–2 feet apart. Begin with your right foot outside the right line and your left foot outside the left line. Jump in the air. Click your heels together and land outside the tape. Keep your hands up and concentrate on quickness—not height—as you jump.

4. **Toe Touch.** The tape is positioned the same as for the Heel Clicks; your starting position is also the same. Jump in the air and land inside the lines with your feet next to each other. Quickly jump again so your feet land outside the lines. Keep your hands at shoulder height and always land inside or outside the lines. Concentrate on quickness rather than height.

5. **Five-Dot Jumping.** Place five dots, or pieces of tape, on the floor. Four dots are the corners of a square and the fifth dot is the middle of the square. Start with your feet on the bottom two dots. Quickly jump and land on the middle dot. Jump again and land on the two top dots. Continue the drill by jumping back to the middle dot and then to the bottom dots. Keep your hands at shoulder height as you jump.

6. **Backboard Touch with Ball.** Start on either side of the basket. Jump up and hit the ball forcefully against the backboard. Always maintain possession of the ball. Land on balance and jump again quickly. This drill can also be done with a weighted basketball.

7. **Long Jump.** Place a 6-foot strip of tape on the floor. Start at the base of the tape and long-jump as far as you can. Use your arms to provide additional power. After landing, shuffle backward to the base of the tape and repeat.

8. **Step-Ups.** Use a step-up board or some type of low step. Step up one foot at a time to the top of the board. Step back down to the floor as quickly as possible and repeat.

9. **Complete the Square.** Start on the baseline at the intersection of the free throw lane line on the left side. Sprint forward to the elbow (intersection of the free throw lane line and the free throw line). Slide across the free throw line to the opposite elbow without crossing your feet. Backpedal down the lane and slide across the baseline to the original starting point. Once reaching the starting point, reverse direction and repeat the drill going the opposite way.

10. **Heavy Rope Jumping.** Use a weighted rope and jump as quickly as you can.

11. **Ricochet Pickups.** Stand 3–5 yards from a wall. Throw the ball underhand at an angle against the wall. Slide laterally to retrieve the ball without crossing your feet. Pick the ball up with two hands and throw it off the wall so that it angles back to your starting position. Work on making quick lateral slides without crossing your feet.

12. **Fingertip Push-Ups.** Execute push-ups on your fingertips. Keep your back straight as you lower yourself to a position where your upper arms are parallel to the floor.

Ballhandling Drills

"Possession of the ball is the best

defense known. Your opponent

can't score if you handle the ball

well."

—Nat Holman, Naismith Basketball
Hall of Fame coach

A good basketball player is able to control the ball without losing possession. Games are often lost as a result of careless turnovers. To improve your game, you must strengthen your hands and arms and improve your ballhandling abilities.

Ballhandling includes the offensive skills of passing, catching, and dribbling. The following drills will help you become a better ball handler:

Stationary Ballhandling Drills

1. **Tap Drill.** Extend your arms and tap the ball quickly between your finger-tips. Start the ball over your head, work down toward the floor, and then back up over your head.

2. **Neck Circles.** Move the ball as quickly as you can around your neck. Change direction.

3. **Waist Circles.** Move the ball around your waist as quickly as you can. Change direction.

4. **Leg Circles.** With your feet shoulder-width apart, move the ball around your right knee. Do the same thing around your left knee. As a variation, put your feet together and work the ball around both legs.

5. **Figure Eight.** Move the ball in a figure-eight pattern through your legs. Change direction.

6. **Straddle Flip.** With your feet shoulder-width apart, hold the ball with both hands in front of your legs, as shown in Photo 18.1. Drop the ball and bring your hands to the back of your legs and catch the ball before it

Photo 18.1 **Straddle Flip (a)**

Photo 18.2 **Straddle Flip (b)**

Photo 18.3 Pretzel (a)

Photo 18.4 Pretzel (b)

hits the floor, as shown in Photo 18.2. Now drop the ball again and catch it in front; continue this action as quickly as possible.

7. **Pretzel.** As shown in Photo 18.3, place one hand on the ball in front of your legs and the other hand on the ball behind your legs. Drop the ball and reverse the position of your hands as shown in Photo 18.4. Continue this action as quickly as you can.

8. **Ricochet.** Stand straight with your feet apart. Bounce the ball hard between your legs and catch it behind you with both hands. Bring the ball in front of your body and repeat.

9. **Run in Place.** Bend over and move your legs in a running pattern, while staying in one place. As shown in Photos 18.5 and 18.6, move the ball behind the right leg with the right hand and then behind the left leg with the left hand. Continue this action, keeping your feet in a straight line.

Photo 18.5 **Run in Place (a)**

Photo 18.6 **Run in Place (b)**

Stationary Dribble Drills

1. **Leg Circles.** With your feet shoulder-width apart, dribble around your right leg using your right hand and left hand. Change direction of your dribble. Do the same thing dribbling around your left leg.

2. **Figure Eight.** Dribble the ball in a figure-eight pattern through your legs. Change direction.

3. **Seesaw.** Assume a wide stance with both hands behind your legs. Bounce the ball from one hand to the other, always keeping the ball behind your legs.

4. **Draw the Picture.** Stand in one spot and dribble the ball in the following shapes: circle, square, and cross. Then dribble in the shapes of various letters of the alphabet. Dribble using your right hand and your left hand.

5. **Front and Back.** Dribble the ball back and forth between your legs using the same hand. Do the same maneuver using the other hand.

6. **Bongo Drill.** As shown in Photo 18.7, get on your knees and dribble the ball as fast as you can, alternating hands like you are playing the bongo drums.

Photo 18.7 **Bongo Drill**

Photo 18.8 **Computer Dribble**

7. **Computer Dribble.** As shown in Photo 18.8, get on your knees and dribble using one finger. Repeat, using all your fingers, including your thumbs.

8. **Dribble Sit-Up.** Lie on your back and dribble the ball by your side. As shown in Photos 18.9 and 18.10, maintain control of your dribble as you execute a sit-up. Dribble using your right hand and then your left hand.

9. **Wall Dribbling.** As shown in Photo 18.11, dribble up and down a wall, bouncing the ball as quickly as you can. Start as high as you can reach,

Photo 18.9 **Dribble Sit-Up (a)**

Photo 18.10 **Dribble Sit-Up (b)**

Photo 18.11 **Wall Dribbling**

go down to chest level, and then back up. Dribble using your right hand and then your left hand.

10. **360-Degree Dribble.** Use your right foot as the pivot foot and dribble in a circle, making front pivots and rear pivots. Dribble using your right hand and then your left hand. Repeat, using your left foot as the pivot foot.

Stationary Two-Ball Dribbling Drills

1. **Control Dribble.** Dribble two balls at the same time and have both balls hit the floor at the same time. As a variation, alternate bounces so that one ball is off the floor when the other hits the floor.

2. **"X" Dribble.** Cross the balls back and forth in front of you. As a variation, dribble and cross the balls behind your back.

3. **Leg Circles.** Dribble one ball around one leg while you dribble the other ball around the other leg. As a variation, dribble two balls in opposite directions around the same leg.

4. **Figure Eight.** Dribble in a figure-eight pattern with both balls going in the same direction. As a variation, dribble in a figure-eight pattern and have the balls going in opposite directions.

Stationary Passing and Catching Drills

1. **Wall Passing—Ball Quickness.** On the wall make a 1-foot square about 4 feet high to serve as your target on air passes. Lower the target when throwing bounce passes. Start approximately 12 feet away from the wall. Pass and catch the ball quickly and accurately. Use different types of passes.
2. **Wall Passing with Fakes.** Use different types of fakes before passing the ball against the wall.

Drills for Dribbling on the Move

1. **Figure-Eight Dribble.** As you walk down the floor, dribble the ball in a figure-eight pattern. As a variation, dribble the ball in the opposite direction in the figure-eight pattern.
2. **Full-Court Dribbling.** Start on the baseline in the triple-threat position as described in Chapter 4. Dribble the length of the court using one of the following types of dribbles: control, speed, change-of-pace, crossover, spin, behind-the-back, or between-the-legs. When you reach the opposite end of the court, use a jump stop followed by a rear pivot. You are now in position to begin the drill again. Drawing on the types of dribbles described in Chapter 9, emphasize different dribbles each workout.
3. **Line Drill.** Starting on the baseline, dribble with the right hand to the free throw line, turn, and dribble back to the baseline using the left hand. Continue by dribbling to half-court with the right hand and then back to the baseline with the left hand. Now dribble to the opposite free throw line with the right hand, come back with the left, and finish the drill by dribbling to the opposite baseline with the right hand and back again with the left hand.
4. **Stop and Go.** Speed dribble from the baseline to the free throw line and stop quickly. Maintain your dribble while you are stopped. Accelerate with a speed dribble to half-court and stop. Accelerate and stop at the free throw line. Finish the drill with a speed dribble to the baseline. You are now at the opposite baseline from where you started. Come back doing the same thing using your other hand.
5. **Slalom Course.** Place cones in a straight line approximately 10 feet apart. Dribble in and out of the cones, always using the hand farthest

from the obstacle. Dribble around the last cone and go through the course again.

6. **Pull-Back, Crossover Dribble.** Using the control dribble, advance two dribbles. Maintain your dribble as you retreat two steps using the pull-back dribble. Cross the ball over to your other hand and do the same thing. Always keep your head up and have your eyes focused on your basket.

7. **Dribble Penetration Drill.** The following dribble moves can be used in this drill: change-of-pace, crossover, inside-out, behind-the-back, and between-the-legs. Start at half-court, dribble hard to the free throw line, execute a dribble move, and drive to the basket for a score. Rebound your shot and advance the ball to half-court, executing a dribble move at the free throw line. Imagine there are defenders at the free throw line. You are using a dribble move to create a scoring opportunity when you are going toward your basket. When you are going toward half-court, you are using a dribble move to get past an opposing player who is playing full-court defense.

Two-Ball Drills for Dribbling on the Move

1. **Straight-Line Dribbling.** Dribble the length of the court, bouncing two balls so they hit the floor at the same time. As a variation, dribble the length of the court alternating bounces. One ball will hit the floor as the other is touching your fingertips.

2. **Zigzag Dribbling.** Dribble the length of the court, using two balls and moving diagonally from side to side. Always keep your head up.

3. **Stop and Go.** Speed dribble using two balls from the baseline to the free throw line and stop quickly. Maintain your dribble while you are stopped. Accelerate with a speed dribble to half-court and stop. Accelerate and then stop at the free throw line. Finish the drill with a speed dribble to the baseline. You are now at the opposite baseline from where you started. Come back to the original starting line using the same routine.

Inside Drills

> "I ask our players to give more of
>
> themselves than they think is
>
> possible. Each time you go beyond
>
> your perceived limit, you become
>
> mentally stronger."
>
> —Pat Summitt, Naismith Basketball
> Hall of Fame coach

Every player must be able to score inside. There are many times during the course of a game when perimeter players can score key points in the post area. Versatile offensive scorers develop both their inside and their outside games.

The following drills will improve your ability to score inside as well as secure offensive rebounds:

1. **Mikan Drill.** This drill is named for Hall of Fame player George Mikan. Mikan stood 6'11" and was professional basketball's first superstar. The Mikan Drill is designed to improve the right-handed and left-handed hook

shot and improve offensive footwork. Start in the middle of the lane, one step from the basket. Take a step, drive the opposite knee up, and shoot a hook shot. Rebound your shot before the ball hits the floor. Take a step and shoot a hook shot on the opposite side. Do not let the ball drop below shoulder level. Continue until you make 15 shots. Another option is to have a partner time you for 30 seconds and record the number of made shots.

2. **Reverse Layups.** Start under the basket with your back to the baseline. Take a step, drive the opposite knee up, and shoot a reverse layup. Rebound the shot and shoot a reverse layup on the opposite side. Continue until you make 15 shots, or see how many you can make in 30 seconds.

3. **Tip Drill.** Start on either side of the basket, throw the ball against the board, and begin tipping it. Use your fingers and wrist to control the ball, keeping your tipping arm fairly straight. At the same time, touch the net with your nontipping hand. Tip the ball eight times and then score. Move to the other side and tip with the opposite hand.

4. **Backboard Touch with Ball.** This drill helps develop strong hands and explosive inside moves. Start on either side of the basket. Jump up and hit the ball forcefully against the backboard, always maintaining possession of the ball. Be balanced as you land and jump again. Continue jumping for five jumps and then score. Move to the other side of the basket and repeat.

5. **Catch Tips.** This drill helps inside players keep the ball high and score quickly. Start on either side of the basket and throw the ball off the board. Rebound with two hands, always keeping the ball above your head. Be balanced when you land and then jump quickly, scoring a basket using a bank shot. Make five baskets and move to the opposite side.

6. **Superman or Superwoman Drill.** This drill improves lateral quickness and hand strength. Start outside the free throw lane, approximately at the block. Throw the ball off the board and retrieve it on the opposite side. Rebound the ball so your feet land outside the free throw lane. Continue going back and forth across the lane for eight rebounds.

7. **Pick-Ups.** This drill requires two players and two balls and is designed to help inside players develop strong inside moves. Place a ball at each free

throw block. The shooter aggressively picks up a ball, makes a power move, and then does the same thing on the opposite side. The second player rebounds the ball and places it back on the floor. The players switch positions after the shooter makes eight shots.

8. **Back-to-the-Basket Moves.** Start under the basket with your back toward the baseline. Throw the ball out to the edge of the free throw lane, slightly higher than the block. Go and get the ball, chin it, and then execute an inside move. Rebound the ball and execute the same move on the opposite side. Work on the following moves: drop step, jump hook, turnaround jump shot, wheel-to-the-middle jump hook, and up and under.

Self-Improvement Training Programs

"Everybody has a will to win. What's

far more important is having the

will to prepare to win."

—Bob Knight, Naismith Basketball
Hall of Fame coach

Mastery of the fundamental skills is vital for basketball success. Outstanding players work individually on their basketball skills year-round. They create sound habits through rigorous, repetitive work.

This chapter presents training programs for both perimeter players and inside players. Always start every training session with a warm-up and stretching exercises. Use straight-line running, "V" cuts, jump stops, and pivots in your warm-up. Every drill listed below has been described in previous chapters.

Perimeter Players Workout 1

1. *Quickness/Agility Drills*

- Speed Rope Jumping
- Line Rope Jumping
- Square Rope Jumping

2. *Ballhandling Drills*

- Ball Slap
- Tap Drill
- Neck Circles
- Waist Circles
- Leg Circles
- Figure Eight
- Wall Passing and Catching

3. *Stationary Dribbling Drills*

- Leg Circles
- Figure Eight
- Front and Back

4. *Dribbling on the Move Drills*

- Figure Eight
- Two-Ball Dribbling
- Full-Court Dribbling (control, speed, and change-of-pace)
- Dribble Penetration Drill (change-of-pace, crossover, inside-out, and behind-the-back)

5. *Perimeter Shooting Drills*

- Nothing but Net
- Bank Shots
- Shoot off the Pass
- Shoot off the Dribble
- Three in a Row
- Beat Michael Jordan
- Game-Winning Free Throws

6. *One-on-One Moves*
- Direct Drive
- Jab Step and Jump Shot
- Hesitation Move
- Crossover Step and Jump Shot

7. *Inside Drills*
- Mikan Drill
- Reverse Layups
- Tip Drill

8. *Free Throws*
- Shoot 50 free throws.

Perimeter Players Workout 2

1. *Quickness/Agility Drills*
- Speed Rope Jumping
- Alternate-Feet Rope Jumping
- Three Jumps and a Double Jump

2. *Ballhandling Drills*
- Ball Slap
- Figure Eight
- Straddle Flip
- Pretzel
- Ricochet
- Run in Place
- Wall Passing and Catching

3. *Stationary Dribbling Drills*
- Leg Circles
- Figure Eight
- Seesaw

4. *Dribbling on the Move Drills*

- Pull-Back, Crossover Dribble
- Line Drill
- Full-Court Dribbling (crossover, spin, behind-the-back, and between-the-legs)
- Dribble Penetration Drill (change-of-pace, crossover, inside-out, and between-the-legs)

5. *Perimeter Shooting Drills*

- Nothing but Net
- Bank Shots
- 25 in a Row
- Shoot off the Pass
- Shoot off the Dribble
- Three in a Row
- Beat Michael Jordan

6. *One-on-One Moves*

- Direct Drive
- Jab Step and Jump Shot
- Crossover Step and Jump Shot
- Rocker Step and Drive
- Step-Back, One-Dribble Jump Shot

7. *Inside Drills*

- Mikan Drill
- Reverse Layups
- Drop Step and Power Move

8. *Free Throws*

- Shoot 50 free throws.

Inside Players Workout 1

1. *Quickness/Agility Drills*

- Speed Rope Jumping
- Line Rope Jumping
- Square Rope Jumping

2. *Ballhandling Drills*

- Ball Slap
- Tap Drill
- Neck Circles
- Waist Circles
- Leg Circles
- Figure Eight
- Wall Passing and Catching

3. *Stationary Dribbling Drills*

- Leg Circles
- Figure Eight
- Front and Back

4. *Dribbling on the Move Drills*

- Full-Court Dribbling (control, speed, and change-of-pace)

5. *Inside Drills*

- Mikan Drill
- Reverse Layups
- Backboard Touch with Ball
- Tip Drill

6. *Post Moves*

- Back-to-the-Basket Moves (drop step, jump hook, turnaround jump shot, wheel-to-the-middle jump hook, and up and under)

7. *Perimeter Shooting Drills*
- Bank Shots
- Shoot off the Pass
- Shoot off the Dribble

8. *Free Throws*
- Shoot 50 Free Throws.

Inside Players Workout 2

1. *Quickness/Agility Drills*
- Speed Rope Jumping
- Alternate-Feet Rope Jumping
- Three Jumps and a Double Jump

2. *Ballhandling Drills*
- Ball Slap
- Figure Eight
- Straddle Flip
- Pretzel
- Ricochet
- Run in Place
- Wall Passing and Catching

3. *Stationary Dribbling Drills*
- Leg Circles
- Figure Eight
- Seesaw

4. *Dribbling on the Move Drills*
- Dribble Penetration Drill (change-of-pace, crossover, behind-the-back, and between-the-legs)
- Pull-Back, Crossover Dribble

5. Inside Drills

- Mikan Drill
- Reverse Layups
- Catch Tips
- Pick-Ups
- Superman or Superwoman Drill

6. Post Moves

- Back-to-the-Basket Moves (drop step, jump hook, turnaround jump shot, wheel-to-the-middle jump hook, and up and under)

7. Perimeter Shooting Drills

- Bank Shots
- 25 in a Row
- Game-Winning Free Throws
- Three in a Row (from the elbow)

8. Free Throws

- Shoot 50 free throws.

Basketball Skills Test

A basketball skills test is a valuable tool to help players recognize their strengths and weaknesses. It identifies specific areas that should be worked on during practice sessions. It also serves as a measuring device as you chart improvement.

This basketball performance profile has been prepared with the assistance of Denny Kuiper, sports communication consultant, and Rhonda Fleming, assistant professor, at Limestone College. The norms are based on an analysis of the performance of men and women participating in basketball activity classes on the college level.

Test Items

60-Second Shooting

Mark a spot on the floor 18 feet from the basket in the middle of the floor. Begin the test by attempting a perimeter shot from the designated shooting spot. Rebound the ball and shoot a layup. Dribble back to the shooting spot. Repeat the procedure of shooting one perimeter shot followed by one layup for a total of 60 seconds. Score two points for every successful perimeter shot and one point for every made layup. Calculate your point total.

60-Second Shooting

Excellent	25 or better
Good	20–24
Average	12–19
Below Average	11 or fewer

Block Jumps

Stand facing the baseline with your feet together and parallel to the free throw block. The free throw block is a term used to describe the marking on the floor that is used to separate opposing players on the free throw lane line. Jump sideways over the block without touching it. Record the number of jumps you make in 30 seconds. Do not count the jump if you land on the free throw block.

Block Jumps

Excellent	90 or better
Good	80–89
Average	60–79
Below Average	59 or fewer

Free Throw Shooting

Shoot 25 free throws and record the number of made shots.

Free Throws

Excellent	19 or better
Good	16–18
Average	11–15
Below Average	10 or fewer

Speed Layups

Place a cone at the top of the free throw circle. Start on the baseline facing the midcourt line. Speed dribble to the top of the free throw circle, go around the cone, and drive to the basket for a layup. Continue for 30 seconds and record the number of successful layups

Speed Layups	
Excellent	7 or better
Good	5–6
Average	3–4
Below Average	2 or fewer

Mikan Drill

Start under the basket and take a short hook shot. Rebound the shot and take a hook shot from the opposite side. Continue alternating sides on every shot. Record the number of shots made in 30 seconds.

Mikan Drill	
Excellent	18 or better
Good	15–17
Average	10–14
Below Average	9 or fewer

Figure-Eight Ballhandling

Start with your feet shoulder-width apart. Place the ball in one hand between your legs. Move it around one leg in a circular motion. Catch it with your other hand and move it around your other leg in the pattern of a figure eight. Record the number of times you bring the ball to the middle (between your legs) in 30 seconds.

Figure-Eight Ballhandling	
Excellent	66 or better
Good	55–65
Average	40–54
Below Average	39 or fewer

Defensive Slides

Start with your outside foot touching the edge of the free throw lane. Using the correct defensive slide, move from one side of the lane to the other. Always touch the free throw lane line with your foot before sliding to the opposite side. Record the number of lines you touch in 30 seconds.

Defensive Slides

Excellent	26 or better
Good	23–25
Average	18–22
Below Average	17 or fewer

Jump and Reach

You will need chalk and a wallboard marked off in feet and inches in order to do this test. Stand sideways next to a wall with the hand farther from the wall resting comfortably. The other arm is raised vertically with the palm facing the wall and the fingers extended. Place chalk dust on the tips of your fingers. Reach as high as possible with the extended arm and record your reaching height in inches. Now crouch and jump as high as possible. Record your jumping height. Your score is determined by subtracting your reaching height from your jumping height. Use the best of three jumps. The Jump and Reach test is recorded in inches.

Jump and Reach

	MEN	WOMEN
Excellent	29 or better	19 or better
Good	26–28	17–18
Average	17–25	12–16
Below Average	16 or under	11 or under

Wall Pass

For this test you need a flat wall space at least 15 feet long and 7 feet high. As shown in Figure A.1, draw two vertical parallel lines on the wall 3 feet apart. Label these lines A and B. Next draw a line on the floor parallel to and 8 feet away from the wall. From this line draw two more parallel lines that each meet the wall at a point 18 inches to the outside of the corresponding wall line. Label these lines A and B so that floor line A is closer to wall line B, and vice versa. The space between wall line A and floor line B will be Area A on the wall; the space between wall line B and floor line A will be Area B.

Begin the test by standing outside of floor line A. Pass the ball to Area A on the wall and run to the outside of floor line B so that you can catch the ball on the rebound. Then throw to Area B on the wall and move back to the outside of floor line A to receive the pass.

Your score is the number of successful passes made in 30 seconds. You may use any type of pass, but do not count passes that hit in the area between wall lines A and B.

Wall Pass

Excellent	22 or better
Good	19–21
Average	14–18
Below Average	13 or fewer

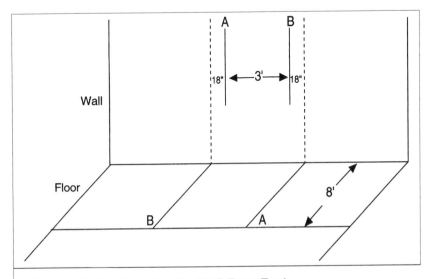

***Figure A.1* Markings for the Wall-Pass Test**

Line Dribble

Begin at the baseline facing the midcourt line. Using your right hand, dribble out to the free throw line. Turn and dribble back to the baseline using your left hand. Then dribble to the midcourt line using your right hand, returning to the baseline with your left. Then dribble to the opposite free throw line with your right hand and finish with a speed dribble back to the baseline with your left hand. Record the number of seconds it takes to complete this course.

Line Dribble	
Excellent	20 seconds or under
Good	20.01–21.00 seconds
Average	21.01–23.00 seconds
Below Average	23.01 seconds or more

The James Naismith Basketball Obstacle Course

An obstacle course provides an opportunity for players to practice skills in a fun and challenging setting. This basketball obstacle course has been developed with assistance from Major Artie Coughlin at the United States Military Academy at West Point. It is called the James Naismith Basketball Obstacle Course.

As shown in Figure B.1, the James Naismith Basketball Obstacle Course has eight stations and is a timed event. Each station was named for a legendary player from the Naismith Memorial Basketball Hall of Fame.

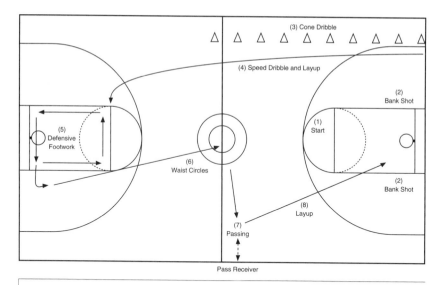

Figure B.1 *James Naismith Basketball Obstacle Course*

Equipment Needed

1. **Two balls.** Place one ball at the free throw block near the start line and place the other in the midcourt circle.

2. **Ten cones.** Place 10 cones on the sideline 5 feet apart, starting from the baseline to the midcourt line.

3. **Pass receiver or toss-back machine.** Position the pass receiver or machine at the intersection of the sideline and the midcourt line.

Stations

1. **"James Naismith" Starting Point.** The starting point for the obstacle course is behind the free throw line facing the basket. A ball is placed on the floor at the free throw block. Be in a ready position. On the command "Go," quickly move to the free throw block and pick up the ball.

2. **"Larry Bird" Bank Shots.** Shoot and make a short bank shot on both sides of the floor. If you miss, get your rebound and go back to the same shooting spot and shoot again. Do not go to the next station until you have made a bank shot on both sides of the floor.

3. **"Bob Cousy" Cone Dribble.** Start on the baseline and dribble in and out of the cones, always using the hand farthest from the cone. Dribble

around the last cone and go through the course again. Finish on the baseline at the original starting point.

4. **"Nate Archibald" Speed Dribble and the "Dr. J" Layup (Julius Erving).** Speed dribble with either hand to the opposite end of the court and make a layup shot. If you miss the shot, get your rebound and shoot another layup. Continue shooting until you score. After making the shot, put the ball on the floor outside the court.

5. **"K. C. Jones" Defensive Footwork.** Start on the baseline at the intersection of the free throw lane line. Sprint forward to the elbow (intersection of the free throw lane line and the free throw line). Slide across the free throw line to the opposite elbow without crossing your feet. Backpedal down the lane and slide across the baseline to the original starting point. Once you reach the starting point, sprint to the midcourt circle. There will be a ball on the floor in the middle of the circle.

6. **"Harlem Globetrotters" Waist Circles.** Pick up the ball and move it around your waist as quickly as you can. Each time the ball passes in front of your midsection, call out the number. After completing five waist circles in one direction, change direction five more times. After completing a total of 10 waist circles, quickly dribble on the midcourt line to a spot 12 feet from a designated pass receiver or toss-back machine.

7. **"Pistol Pete" Passing (Pete Maravich).** Make five accurate and crisp passes to the receiver positioned at the intersection of the sideline and the midcourt line. Call out the number after each pass. On the fifth pass, catch the ball and dribble to the basket at the end of the court where you started the obstacle course.

8. **"Magic Johnson" Game-Winning Layup.** Complete the obstacle course by making a layup shot. Your time for the obstacle course ends as the ball goes through the net.

Checklist for Offensive Fundamentals

This is a summary of the key teaching points for each offensive fundamental. The following checklists can serve as a guide for improving your basketball skills.

Triple-Threat Position

- Feet are shoulder-width apart and knees are bent.
- All joints are flexed and your body weight is evenly distributed.
- The ball is positioned near the dominant shoulder.
- Shoulders are facing your basket.
- Eyes are looking at the basket and seeing the entire floor.
- From this position, you can shoot, pass, or dribble.

Perimeter Shooting

- Feet are shoulder-width apart with the shooting foot slightly in front.
- Toes are pointed at the basket.
- Shooting hand is centered on the ball.
- Balance hand is positioned on the side of the ball.
- Eyes are focused on the target before, during, and after the shot attempt.
- The shot is initiated with your legs.
- Ball is cocked in the shooting pocket.
- Elbow is in front of the wrist and pointed at the basket.
- Elbow is kept under the ball.
- Fingers are thrust up and forward through the ball.
- Angle of release on the shot is 60 degrees.
- Head is kept still during the shot.
- The ball has backspin during the shot.
- Follow-through is done with complete elbow extension and wrist flexion.

Layup Shot

- Head is up and eyes are looking at the target.
- Dribble with the hand away from the defender.
- Bring the nondribbling hand to the ball and take it up with two hands.
- Jump off the inside foot and drive the other leg and knee up in the air.
- Release the ball at the top of the jump.
- Shoot the ball softly off the top corner of the backboard square.

Free Throw Shooting

- Establish a routine.
- Set feet shoulder-width apart with the shooting foot slightly in front.
- Slightly bend knees.
- Bounce the ball a set number of times.
- Place your shooting hand in the center of the ball.
- Cock the ball in the shooting pocket.
- Concentrate on your target.
- Keep your elbow in.
- Initiate the shot with your legs.

- Extend the shooting arm in a smooth, fluid motion.
- Release the ball high.
- Hold your follow-through.

Passing

- See the defense and your offensive teammate before passing.
- Make accurate and crisp passes.
- Pass the ball away from the defense.
- Deliver the pass when the receiver is open.
- Do not wind up when you pass.
- Pass through or past a defender.
- Keep two hands on the ball until the pass is made.
- Use fakes to open passing lanes.

Catching

- Keep your hands above your waist and give a target to the passer.
- Meet each pass.
- Keep your eyes on the ball into your hands.
- Catch the ball with two hands.
- After receiving the pass, look at your basket and bring the ball into the triple-threat position.

Dribbling

- Always dribble with a purpose.
- Keep your head up and see the floor.
- Dribble with the hand farthest from the defender.
- Keep the nondribbling arm up for protection.
- Cup the dribbling hand and spread the fingers comfortably.
- The dribble is a push-pull motion of the arm, wrist, and fingers.
- The fingers and the pads of the hand control the ball.
- Never pick up your dribble without a pass or a shot.

Starting

- Lower your shoulder and lean your head in the direction you wish to go.
- Step with your lead foot first.

- Push hard off your foot.
- Maintain body lean when starting forward.
- Use a quick, pumping action of the arms.

Stopping

- Land with your knees bent.
- Keep your head up and centered over your body.
- Maintain a wide base of support.
- Keep the back fairly straight without bending at the waist.

Pivoting

- Keep the feet shoulder-width apart and the knees bent.
- Keep your head up and centered over your body.
- Pivot by lifting up the heel and turning on the ball of your pivot foot.

Glossary

Assist   A pass from an offensive player to a teammate that results in an immediate score

Back screen   A move by an offensive player away from the basket to set a screen for a teammate

Backboard   The flat, rectangular board placed behind the basket

Backcourt   That half of the court that is the farthest from the offensive basket; also, the position played by the guards

Backdoor cut   A cut behind the defender toward the basket against a defensive overplay

Ball screen   A screen on the defender guarding the offensive player with the ball

Ball side   The side of the court on which the ball is located; also called the *strong side*

Bank shot   A shot in which the ball strikes the backboard and then rebounds into the basket

Baseball pass   A one-handed pass used to advance the ball up the court

Baseline   The out-of-bounds line underneath either basket on both ends of the floor; also called the *endline*

Basket   A goal that results in a score; also, the rim through which the ball is thrown

Behind-the-back dribble   A dribble behind the body from one hand to the opposite hand

Behind-the-back pass   A pass thrown behind the back

Between-the-legs dribble   A dribble through the legs from one hand to the opposite hand

Block out   A rebounding position with the rebounder making contact and staying between the basket and the opponent

Bounce pass   A pass that hits the floor between the passer and the receiver

Catch and face   A technique for receiving a pass and squaring up to the basket in the triple-threat position

Center   Often the tallest player on a team; normally plays close to the basket and is responsible for securing rebounds and blocking shots

Change-of-pace dribble   Alternately slowing down and speeding up the dribble in order to penetrate past a defender

Chest pass   A two-handed pass thrown from the chest

Chin it   The position of the ball after a rebound; the ball is directly under the chin with the elbows and fingers up

Clear out   An offensive tactic in which an offensive player leaves an area so the ball handler has more room to maneuver

Clock-down cut   A cut by the help-side forward toward the baseline as the ball handler drives to the basket

Control dribble   A low dribble used when closely guarded

Crossover dribble   A dribble from one hand to the opposite hand across and in front of the body

Crossover step   An offensive move consisting of a jab step followed with a step in the opposite direction

Cross screen   A lateral move by an offensive player to set a screen for a teammate

Curl cut   A cut off a screen toward the basket; used when the defender is trailing the cutter

Cut   An offensive move used to create an advantage; usually made toward the basket, ball, or a teammate

Defense   The act of attempting to prevent your opponent from scoring

Down screen   A move by an offensive player toward the baseline to set a screen for a teammate

Dribble drive   Dribbling in a straight line to the basket

Dribbler   An offensive player who moves the ball on the court by legally bouncing it with one hand

Dunk   A basket made by driving or slamming the ball through the basket from above the rim

Early offense   The transition period between the fast break and a team's half-court offense

Elbow   The area of the court where the free throw line and the free throw lane line intersect

Endline   See *Baseline*

Fade cut   A cut used by an offensive player coming off a screen when the defender is in a sagging position

Fake   A technique used to get a defensive player off balance or out of position

Fast break   An offensive tactic in which a team rapidly moves the ball the length of the court by means of long passes and/or quick dribble drives in an attempt to score before the opponent can set up its defense

Field goal   A basket made while the ball is in play

Field goal percentage   The number of field goals made divided by the number of field goals attempted

Fishhook cut   See *Shallow cut*

Forwards   Two players generally positioned closer to the basket than the guards; they often assume a floor position along the perimeters of the free throw lane and maneuver both inside and outside

Free throw   An unguarded attempt to score from a line 15 feet from the basket

Free throw block   The marking on the floor that is used to separate opposing players on the free throw lane line

Free throw percentage   The number of free throws made divided by the number of free throws attempted

Front pivot   Moving forward while turning on the pivot foot

Frontcourt   The offensive area of the court from the midcourt line to the baseline; also, the positions played by the forwards and center

Give-and-go   An offensive maneuver, sometimes called an *inside cut,* whereby a player passes to a teammate and cuts for the basket looking for a return pass

Guards   The two players who typically move the ball from the backcourt into the frontcourt and then position themselves farthest from the basket

Help side   The side of the court opposite that of the ball; also called the *weak side*

High post   An area of the court located near the free throw line

High-side post defense   The floor location of a defender guarding a post player when the defensive player is positioned between the midcourt line and the post player and the offensive player with the ball is located at the wing

Inside cut   A cut used by an offensive player who passes the ball to a teammate and cuts to the basket looking for a return pass

Jab step   A small step toward the defensive player with the nonpivot foot

Jump shot   An offensive shot in which the offensive player's feet leave the floor

Jump stop   Coming to a full stop by jumping off one foot and landing in a parallel or a staggered stance with both feet hitting the floor at the same time; also called a *quick stop*

"L" cut   A cut in the shape of the letter "L" that is used when the defender is in the passing lane but is playing very loosely

Layup shot   A close-in shot made when moving to the basket

Loading the gun   Placing the ball in the shooting pocket with the wrist cocked ready to shoot

Low post   An area of the court located near the basket

Low-side post defense   The floor location of a defender guarding a post player when the defensive player is positioned between the baseline and the post player and the offensive player with the ball is located at the wing

Midcourt line   The line in the middle of the court that separates the frontcourt from the backcourt; also called the *10-second line*

Offense   The team that has possession of the ball

One-two stop   See *Stride stop*

Outlet pass   A pass made from a rebounder to an offensive teammate

Overhand layup shot   A layup shot with the shooting hand positioned on the back of the ball with the palm facing the basket

Overhead pass   A pass made while the ball is held above the head with both hands

Paint   The area inside the free throw lane

Passing lane   The area between two offensive players where a pass could be made

Penetration   When the ball is dribbled or passed inside the defensive area toward the basket

Pick   See *Screen*

Pick-and-roll   A play in which an offensive player screens for the ball handler and then rolls toward the basket; also referred to as a *screen and roll*

Pivot   The rotation of the body around one foot that is kept in a stationary position

Point guard   Usually a team's floor leader who initiates the offense and controls the tempo of the game

Post area   The area around the free throw lane

Post player   The position usually played by the center

Post up   An offensive position close to, and facing away from, the basket in preparation to receive a pass

Power forward   Usually the bigger, stronger forward who plays close to the basket and is responsible for rebounding and inside scoring

Power layup shot   A layup used when closely guarded

Pull-back dribble   A retreat dribble used to avoid defensive pressure or traps

Push pass   A pass used to pass through or past a defender who is guarding closely

Quick stop   See *Jump stop*

Ready position   Stance with the knees bent, the hands up and ready, and the head up and looking forward

Rear pivot   A move that involves stepping backward while turning on the pivot foot; also called a *reverse pivot*

Rebound   Securing the ball off the backboard or the rim after a missed shot attempt

Reverse dribble   See *Spin dribble*

Reverse pivot   See *Rear pivot*

Rocker step   An offensive move consisting of a jab step followed by a step backward and then a long step past the defender

Sagging defense   When a defender plays loosely and does not pressure the offensive player

Screen   An offensive technique used to block or delay an opponent from reaching a desired floor position; also called a *pick*

Screen and roll   See *Pick-and-roll.*

Second shot   Offensive shot taken after gaining an offensive rebound

Shallow cut   A change-of-direction cut that takes the shape of a fishhook and is used as a pressure release; also called a *fishhook cut*

Shape up   A term used to describe the movement of the screener toward the ball after the screen has been set

Shooting guard   Generally, the player who takes the majority of the shots from the perimeter, many of which are three-point attempts

Shooting pocket   The area of the body under a player's dominant shoulder where a shot is initiated; it is the triple-threat ball position

Small forward   A player who is usually bigger than the guards but smaller than the power forward; responsibilities include both inside and outside work

Spacing   The positioning of the offensive players, who should be approximately 15 to 18 feet from one another

Speed dribble   A high, quick dribble used to advance the ball up the court when there are no defenders blocking your path

Spin dribble   A change-of-direction dribble move utilizing a rear pivot; also called a *reverse dribble*

Stride stop   Coming to a full stop by landing on one foot first and then the other foot; also called the *one-two stop*

Strong side See *Ball side*

Switch A defensive tactic of changing the offensive players being guarded by the defenders

10-second line See *Midcourt line*

Three-point shot A field goal attempt from outside the three-point line

Transition Changing from defense to offense and vice versa

Trap A defensive tactic in which two players double-team the ball handler

Triple-threat position An offensive position from which the ball handler can either shoot, pass, or dribble

Turnover An error or mistake that causes the offensive team to lose possession of the ball

Underhand layup shot A layup shot with the shooting hand in front and under the ball

"V" cut A fake in one direction and movement in the opposite direction in order to get open for a pass

Weak side See *Help side*

Wing A perimeter position on the side of the basket outside the free throw line

References

Bee, Clair. *Drills and Fundamentals.* New York: A.S. Barnes & Co., 1942.

Bird, Larry. *Bird on Basketball.* Reading, MA: Addison-Wesley Publishing Company, 1988.

Carril, Pete. *The Smart Take from the Strong.* New York: Simon & Schuster, 1997.

Gibbons, Tim (ed). *The Path to Excellence: A Comprehensive View of Development of U.S. Olympians Who Competed from 1984 to 1998.* Initial Report: Results of the Talent Identification and Development Questionnaire to U.S. Olympians, Athletic Development and Coaching and Sport Sciences Divisions, 2002.

Hill, Andrew. *Be Quick but Don't Hurry!* New York: Simon & Schuster, 2001.

Holman, Nat. *Holman on Basketball.* New York: Crown Publishers, 1950.

Howell, Bailey. "Offensive Rebounding." *Basketball Bulletin.* Winter 1980.

Jordan, Michael. *I Can't Accept Not Trying.* New York: HarperCollins Publishers, 1994.

Kellner, Stan. *Beyond the Absolute Limit.* Brooklyn: Ropp Press, 1995.

Knight, Bob. *Knight: My Story.* New York: St. Martin's Press, 2002.

Knight, Bob, and Pete Newell. *Basketball According to Knight and Newell* (vol. II). Seymour, IN: Graessle-Mercer Co., 1986.

Krause, Jerry, Don Meyer, and Jerry Meyer. *Basketball Skills & Drills.* Champaign: Human Kinetics, 1999.

Krause, Jerry, and Ralph L. Pim. *Coaching Basketball.* Chicago: Contemporary Books, 2002.

McGuire, Frank. *Team Basketball Offense and Defense.* New York: Prentice-Hall, 1966.

Robertson, Oscar. *The Art of Basketball.* Los Angeles: Oscar Robertson Media Ventures, 1998.

Rupp, Adolph. *Rupp's Championship Basketball.* New York: Prentice-Hall, 1948.

Sharman, Bill. *Sharman on Basketball Shooting.* Englewood Cliffs, NJ: Prentice-Hall, 1970.

Summitt, Pat. *Reach for the Summit.* New York: Broadway Books, 1998.

Taylor, Fred. "Rebounding Fundamentals." *Coaches' All-American "Reboundome" Drills,* p. 5. Roxton, TX: Korney Board Aids, 1974.

Valvano, Jim. "Off-Season Fundamentals." 1980 *Medalist Notebook* (vol. vi). Mequon, WI: Medalist Industries, Inc., 1980.

Vernacchia, Ralph A. *Inner Strength: The Mental Dynamics of Athletic Performance.* Palo Alto, CA: Warde Publishers, 2003.

Williams, Pat. *Go for the Magic.* Nashville: Thomas Nelson Publishers, 1995.

—— . *How to Be Like Mike: Life Lessons About Basketball's Best.* Deerfield Beach, FL: Health Communications, 2001.

Wissel, Hal. *Basketball Steps to Success.* Champaign, IL: Human Kinetics, 1994.

Wolff, Alexander. "The American Athlete, Age 10." *Sports Illustrated,* p. 68 (2003, October 6).

Wooden, John R. *Practical Modern Basketball.* New York: The Ronald Press Co., 1966.

—— . *Wooden: A Lifetime of Observations and Reflections On and Off the Court.* Chicago: Contemporary Books, 1997.

Woods, Ernie. "Offensive Rebounding Techniques and Methods." 2002. Retrieved from www.cybersportsusa.com/hooptactics/coaching/coachdefault.asp.

Index

Page numbers in italics refer to photos and diagrams.

About the Author

Ralph Pim is an assistant professor in the Department of Physical Education at the United States Military Academy at West Point. He serves as the director of instructional administration and is a basketball sport educator.

Pim has coached and taught basketball at the secondary and collegiate levels for 30 years. As a collegiate head coach, Pim built Alma (MI) College and Limestone (SC) College into highly successful programs. His Alma teams were ranked nationally for points scored and three-point field goals, and the 1989 squad recorded the school's best overall record in 47 years. He also coached at Central Michigan, William and Mary, Northwestern Louisiana, and Barberton (OH) High School. Barberton won the 1976 Ohio State Championship and was selected the seventh best team in the country.

Pim spent 10 years as the technical advisor for the Basketball Association of Wales. He implemented training programs to facilitate the development of basketball in that country and assisted with the training of their national teams. He is a member of the National Association of Basketball Coaches and serves on the Champions of Character Committee for the NAIA.

Pim has authored numerous coaching articles and is the coeditor of *Coaching Basketball*. He is also the coauthor of *Lessons from the Legends*, a three-book series about Naismith Hall of Fame coaches. Pim is a graduate of Springfield (MA) College. He earned his master's degree from Ohio State University and his doctorate from Northwestern Louisiana State University.